THE TOP
ONE HUNDRED
CHINESE DISHES

THE TOP ONE HUNDRED CHINESE DISHES

KENNETH LO

TEN SPEED PRESS
Berkeley, California

THE TOP ONE HUNDRED CHINESE DISHES

First published in Australasia in 1992 by
Simon & Schuster Australia
20 Barcoo Street, East Roseville NSW 2069

A Paramount Communications Company
Sydney New York London Toronto Tokyo Singapore

TEN SPEED PRESS
P.O. Box 7123
Berkeley, California 94707

Illustrations © 1992 by Helen Semmler
Cover and text design by Helen Semmler
Typeset in Australia by Asset Typesetting Pty Ltd
Book production by South China Printing Co. Ltd, Hong Kong

ISBN 0-89815-497-9

Library of Congress Cataloguing-in-Publication Data

Lo, Kenneth H. C.
   The top one hundred Chinese dishes / Ken Lo.
      p.   cm.
   Includes index.
   ISBN 0-89815-497-9
   1. Cookery, Chinese. I. Title.
TX724.5.C5L626 1992
641.5951 - - dc20   92-12158
                                                     CIP

Printed in Hong Kong
1 2 3 4 5 / 96 95 94 93 92

CONTENTS

Introduction   6

Glossary   8

The Chinese Kitchen   10

Soup   14

Rice and Noodles   28

Vegetables,
Beancurd and Eggs   50

Fish and Seafood   84

Chicken and Duck   102

Meat   120

Index   143

INTRODUCTION

ONE OF THE MOST remarkable things about China today is that even though it has a population of over a billion people, the majority of them are reasonably well fed. This has been possible only because of intensive labour and flexible use and cultivation of agricultural products. In the north and north-west, people cultivate and consume wheat, corn and maize. Along the Yangzi (Yangtze) River, the main agricultural produce is rice, which is produced in three crops a year in the southern semi-tropical provinces such as Guangdong (Kwangtung). In the mountainous areas of the coastal south-east, sweet potatoes are grown to supplement the rice.

For the average Chinese family meal, these grains are supplemented by vegetables and small amounts of meat, poultry, fish and seafood. A home-cooked Chinese meal is thus both extremely economical and healthy.

A few years ago I wrote a book entitled *Cheap Chow* (in the United States it was called *Chinese Cooking on Next to Nothing*). When it was launched in London by my publisher, we threw a party which was attended by nearly 100 journalists, where the Chinese food served cost a total of UK £15 (A$37/US$30).

While many very appetizing and nourishing dishes can be cheap, one should be aware that some Chinese meals can also be among the most expensive in the world, either because the ingredients can only be harvested in small quantities or because they require a lot of preparation. Recently an American magazine, the *Smithsonian*, reported that the top grade bird's nest used for the famous Chinese soup was valued at US$600 per ounce (A$27 per gram/ UK£300 per ounce) — slightly dearer than gold! Hence Chinese food is one of the very few classical cuisines of the world which can be enjoyed both by people of affluence and those of the most modest of means.

The top 100 Chinese dishes are not necessarily the most expensive or the cheapest in the cuisine. Instead, they are those dishes that are most reminiscent of the flavour of life and food in China, and the most likely to appeal to people of other countries as well.

With this loose definition as my guideline, I have brought together my favourites among the most popular Chinese dishes I have encountered, both in China and abroad, in over three-quarters of a century — the length of time that I have been eating Chinese food!

GLOSSARY

B

BAMBOO SHOOTS: available fresh, canned and dried. The canned variety should be rinsed prior to use and the dried should be soaked

BARBECUED PORK: Cantonese, Cha Shao

BEAN SPROUTS: available fresh and canned

BEAN THREAD (TRANSPARENT) NOODLES: made from the flour of mung beans; soak in hot water for 15-30 minutes before cooking, cook until tender

BEANCURD: also called tofu; made from soya bean purée which is filtered for its milk, then cooked until set into a firm, custard-like texture

BEEF SHIN: shank

C

CAPSICUM: red capsicum (bell pepper), green capsicum (bell pepper)

CHILLI SAUCE: made from chillies, sugar and vinegar

CHILLIES: fresh red or green chillies, dried red chillies

CHINESE (CELERY) CABBAGE: also called Nappa or Napa cabbage, Tientsin cabbage, Shantung cabbage, Michihli cabbage, wong nga bok choy, or wong bok; long and pale green in colour, the leaves are curled at the edges and tightly wrapped around a central head

CHINESE MUSHROOM SAUCE: made from mushrooms and soya beans

CORIANDER: see fresh coriander

CORNFLOUR: cornstarch

D

DRIED BLACK MUSHROOMS: also called dried shiitakes; usually soaked 30 minutes in hot water

DRIED HAIR VEGETABLE: also called sea moss

DRIED LILY BUDS: also called golden needles; dried flower buds of the tiger lily

DRIED PRAWNS: dried shrimps; usually soaked in hot water for 10 minutes

DRIED WHEAT OR EGG NOODLES: cook 2-20 minutes in boiling water (depending on thickness) or until tender

E

EGG WHITE: lightly beaten and used for dipping

EGGPLANT, ITALIAN: also called aubergine

F

FERMENTED BEANCURD: also known as Chinese cheese; beancurd fermented in chillies, wine and spices

FRESH CORIANDER: also called cilantro or Chinese parsley

FRESH RICE FLOUR NOODLES: need no soaking or precooking; cook by steaming or stir-frying until heated through

FRESH WHEAT OR EGG NOODLES: usually cooked in boiling water for 30-60 seconds for thin noodles, 2-4 minutes for thick noodles, or until tender

FRYING PAN: alternative to the wok

G

GINGKO NUTS: also called white nuts. Edible nuts from the gingko tree; available fresh, canned or dry. Remove the bitter core before use

GREEN MUSTARD PICKLES: mustard greens preserved in a spicy brine

H

HOISIN SAUCE: made from soya beans, chillies, sugar and salt

P

PAN: either a wok or a frying pan

PORK BELLY: also called fresh bacon or side pork

PORK KNUCKLE: also called hock; if not available use fresh ham or boneless butt or shoulder

PORK TROTTERS: pigs' feet

PRAWNS: shrimps; shell and devein before cooking

R

RICE-STICK NOODLES: cook 1-5 minutes in boiling water, or until transparent

RICE WINE: also called Chinese rice wine, or Shaoxing (shao-hsing) rice wine

RICE WINE VINEGAR: made from Chinese rice wine

S

SALTED BLACK BEANS: also called fermented black beans

SHIN: shank

SHRIMP SAUCE: available dried and in liquid form

SICHUAN HOT BEAN PASTE: made from soya paste, chillies and oil

SICHUAN PRESERVED VEGETABLES: Chinese radish, chillies and spices in brine

SOYA SAUCE: available in two varieties — light and dark; light soya sauce is used mainly for vegetables and is thinner and lighter than dark soya sauce

SPRING ONIONS: also called scallions

T

TOFU: see beancurd

W

WINTER PICKLES: also called pickled cabbage; yellow to green in colour; available canned or in jars

MISCELLANEOUS

Measurements: The following approximate US alternative amounts are used:

100 mL = ½ cup	600 mL = 2⅔ cups
150 mL = ⅔ cup	900 mL = 4 cups
300 mL = 1⅓ cups	1 L = 4 cups
400 mL = 1¾ cups	1-2 L = 4¾ cups
450 mL = 2 cups	

THE CHINESE KITCHEN

NO MORE THAN two or three decades ago, most of the cooking in China was done on wood, charcoal, or coal fires. Nowadays, the Chinese kitchen is beginning to resemble the Western kitchen — most urban cooking is done on gas — however, the average Chinese kitchen is still much more simply equipped. We employ far fewer gadgets: hardly any kitchen has a blender or a microwave oven. Normally, there isn't even an oven so Peking Duck, like other dishes that require roasting, cannot be cooked in an ordinary Chinese kitchen (in China it is available only in restaurants specializing in Peking Duck)! Ironically, Peking Duck can be more conveniently cooked in a suburban kitchen in London or Melbourne than in Beijing (Peking) itself.

THE WOK

THE WOK WAS probably first developed and used in China from the fourth to the second centuries BC. It has only recently become a popular cooking utensil in the West. As more dishes have been cooked in the wok than in any other kitchen utensil in the world, I feel that I should not fail to emphasise it as an important piece of equipment in the Chinese kitchen. It became popular because it could be used over an open fire. As well as being the best pan for stir-frying, it can also be used as a steamer (by adding boiling water and a round bamboo basket steamer); as a shallow-fryer; as a deep-fryer; as a double boiler; for braising and stewing; and for slow simmering.

Stir-frying is a form of Chinese cooking which has become extremely popular in the West. One of the easiest (and worst) habits to get into when stir-frying is simply to throw all the ingredients into the wok and stir them over high heat. What you get if you do this is a dish of mish-mash! To avoid this, remember the following general principles of stir-frying. As a rule, stir-frying is done in two stages. First, the main ingredients are cut into pieces — diced into small cubes, or cut into thin slices or matchsticks — and are then cooked either over high heat to seal the food quickly, so that it will retain most of its natural juices, or over medium heat to retain the tenderness of the food. After this, the main ingredients are pushed to one side away from the high heat or removed from the wok. The supplementary ingredients are then cooked at the centre of the wok where the heat is the highest. It is only in the final stage that the lightly cooked main ingredients are returned to the hot centre of the wok to finish cooking with the supplementary ingredients in one short blaze of heat.

Sauces in China are not meant to dominate the other ingredients in a dish, but rather to enhance them and to complement the flavours of the foods that are the mainstay of the meal (rice, noodles, steam buns, pancakes, etc). The last-minute addition of stock, soya sauce or other liquids during stir-frying creates unique Chinese sauces. Although these sauces may be nameless, they make a significant contribution to Chinese cuisine.

THE STEAMER

ANOTHER PROMINENT FEATURE of the Chinese kitchen is the steamer; it is used much more frequently in Chinese cooking than in Western cuisine. This is due to the lack of ovens and also because rice is cooked in such quantities and with such regularity that the resulting steam (especially in cooking congee, or soft rice) is an important heat source. The Chinese steamer is usually a bamboo basket attached to the top of a rice boiler. It is often made in several layers so that the dishes which require the most heat can be placed in the basket nearest the boiling water, and those which require the least heat can go in the top basket. The lid of the steamer is made of woven strips of bamboo, which enables the rising steam to pass through, rather than condensing and dripping into the food being cooked.

For dishes that require a lengthy cooking time, the steamer can be used as a double boiler. If the water in the boiler is replenished with regularity, the cooking can go on indefinitely. There are a number of Chinese meat dishes, usually prepared from tough cuts such as beef shin (shank), pork trotters (pigs' feet), and pork knuckle (hock) which are cooked to a jelly-like tenderness and are considered prized delicacies! Generally, we Chinese make only a few long-cooked dishes in the steamer. These are accompanied by one or two stir-fried dishes that have been cooked at the last moment. After all, one aim of the Chinese chef is to serve a variety of dishes which have been cooked in different ways.

In every Chinese kitchen there is usually a stockpot simmering away on the stove. Chinese stock is made by boiling chicken carcasses. To produce a richer stock, the Chinese add a duck carcass and pork knuckle (hock) or bones. They may also add 125-250 grams (¼-½ lb) of minced raw chicken breast to 1.2-1.8 litres (2-3 pt) of stock to cook for 4-5 minutes before straining. This adds strength as well as freshness. In China such a stock is termed Superior Broth, and is added when a strong stock is required to make flavourful sauces and vegetable dishes.

The other distinctive difference between the Western and Chinese kitchens is that the Chinese use a heavy chopping board and cleavers. The board should be a thick block from a tree trunk about 10-15 centimetres (4-6 in) thick, with the grains of the wood running vertically. It is important that the wood grains run vertically so that pieces of the board do not become chipped and mixed into the food.

Chinese cleavers are extraordinarily sharp and heavy.

They are used for all kinds of cutting including slicing, dicing, mincing and carving. Once you learn to use them you will never want to use knives of a normal weight.

In the end, however, you do not require any Chinese equipment at all to cook the dishes in this book. You can cut with ordinary knives (as long as they are sharp) and chop on ordinary chopping boards. You do not even need a wok. Instead you can use a deep non-stick frying pan. If it is difficult for you to approximate the high heat of a wok on your stove, allow the oil in the pan an extra half-minute over the heat before adding the food. This initial sizzling and searing is important in maintaining flavour in stir-frying.

If you are really interested in Chinese food and cooking, your Western kitchen can easily become a Chinese kitchen. I have cooked for twenty years in a domestic Western kitchen, and my only Chinese equipment is a couple of cleavers and a chopping board!

SOUP

SOUP

SOUPS PLAY A different role in a Chinese meal than in a Western one. Chinese soups are usually not separate courses; instead they are drunk in individual spoonfuls throughout the meal. Towards the end of the meal, the last of the soup is frequently poured into the rice bowl to wash down the remaining food and grains of rice. These soups tend to be clear rather than heavy and thick.

This does not mean, however, that there are no thick soups in the Chinese repertoire. I suspect that many of these are legacies from earlier periods of Chinese culinary history. About 2000 years ago, before flour was widely used for making noodles and cakes, most Chinese cooking consisted of boiling meat, grains and vegetables into a thick stew. This ancient stew, called *keng*, became the accepted meal for all classes. Still eaten today as a simple, inexpensive and filling dish, *keng* may have been the original thick soup in China. Over the centuries, starchy foods such as rice and noodles began to be cooked as separate courses. The clear communal soup thus serves to replace the liquid element of *keng*.

EGG-FLOWER SOUP

Dan Hua Tang

*900 mL (1½ pt) strong chicken
   stock
2 eggs, well beaten
1 tablespoon light soya sauce
¾ teaspoon sesame oil
1-1½ tablespoons finely chopped
   spring onions (scallions)
Salt to taste
Pepper to taste*

3-4 portions

ONE OF THE MOST commonly prepared and consumed soups in China is Egg-Flower Soup, or Egg Drop Soup. It is popular because it is quick and easy to prepare.

Although the ingredients used in this soup are few and simple, the green of the spring onions and the yellow of the eggs make it quite attractive.

Method: Bring the stock to a gentle boil in a large pan. Slowly pour the beaten eggs through the prongs of a fork onto the surface of the gently simmering stock. Add the soya sauce. Stir after the eggs have set.

Serving: Pour the soup into a large serving bowl for the diners to help themselves. Sprinkle the top of the soup with sesame oil and chopped spring onions. Season with salt and pepper to taste.

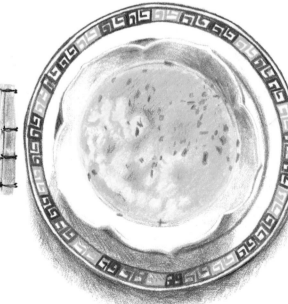

HOT AND SOUR SOUP
Suan La Tang

8 medium dried black mushrooms
1.2 L (4 cups) strong beef stock
4 tablespoons wood ear fungus
2 cakes beancurd (tofu)
120-150 g (4-5 oz) cooked and
   shredded chicken meat
90 g (3 oz) Sichuan pickles
1 egg, beaten
2 tablespoons green peas
1 tablespoon chopped spring onions
   (scallions)

SAUCE
1¼ tablespoons cornflour
   (cornstarch), blended with
   6 tablespoons water
2 tablespoons light soya sauce
Ground black pepper to taste
4-6 tablespoons rice wine vinegar

4-6 portions

HOT AND SOUR SOUP is a popular Chinese winter soup made from strong stock. Basic Beef Broth (page 22) is admirably suited to this purpose.

Method: Soak mushrooms in 5-6 tablespoons of hot water for 30 minutes. Reserve the mushroom water. Remove stems and cut caps into quarters. Add mushrooms and mushroom water to the stock. Bring to the boil and let stand in the hot water for 15 minutes. Soak wood ears in hot water for 5 minutes, rinse and drain. Cut beancurd into 2 cm (¾ in) cubes. Add beancurd cubes, chicken, pickles, wood ears, peas and spring onions to the mushrooms. Bring to the boil. Pour the beaten egg in a stream slowly and evenly over the surface of the soup. Stir when the egg has set.

   To make the sauce, combine all the ingredients in a bowl until well mixed. Pour it slowly into the simmering soup. This will thicken the soup and make it pronouncedly spicy.

Serving: Serve in individual soup bowls. In north and west China, a separate bowl of vinegar, ground black pepper, finely chopped chillis and sesame oil is set on the table for the diners to add to their soup if they want more spice.

CHICKEN SOUP WITH NOODLES
Ji Tang Mian

*Approximately 225-300 g
  (8-10 oz) thin fresh egg noodles
  or vermicelli
180-240 g (6-8 oz) cooked boneless
  chicken
180-240 g (6-8 oz) ham
8 tablespoons finely chopped spring
  onions (scallions)
1.5 L (6 cups) strong chicken stock
Salt to taste
Pepper to taste*

5-6 portions

I HAVE CLASSIFIED Chicken Soup with Noodles as one of the top Chinese soups because it is an extremely popular appetizer for receptions or dinner parties. It is used, as sherry or champagne is used in the West, to welcome guests — the first thing to warm the "cockles" of the visitor's heart.

This very simple dish consists of boiled noodles in chicken broth. Garnish with a small amount of shredded chicken and shredded ham and a pinch of finely chopped spring onion.

Method: Cook the noodles or vermicelli by boiling them in ample water for 30 to 60 seconds or until tender. Drain and divide them equally among 5-6 bowls. Cut chicken and ham into matchsticks. Sprinkle them over the noodles. Sprinkle the contents of each bowl with a large pinch of chopped spring onions.

Heat chicken stock in a saucepan. Season with salt and pepper if necessary.

Serving: Just before serving, bring stock to the boil, then pour it evenly over the noodles and garnishing ingredients. Serve immediately.

This dish of noodles must be served hot to convey a warm welcome.

CHICKEN AND MUSHROOM SOUP

Dong Gu Ji Tang

*8-10 medium dried black
   mushrooms*
*250 g (½ lb) boneless chicken
   breast*
Salt to taste
*2 tablespoons cornflour
   (cornstarch)*
1 egg white, lightly beaten
3 tablespoons vegetable oil
8 medium fresh mushrooms
*750 mL (3 cups) strong chicken
   stock*
2 slices root ginger
Pepper to taste
1½ tablespoons light soya sauce

4-5 portions

AGAINST THE DARK brown soup, the slices of chicken coated in egg white and cornflour appear resplendently white. The mushroom flavour blends easily and naturally with the neutral savouriness of the chicken in this attractive soup.

I well remember being with my mother at the famous Hsing-Ya restaurant in Shanghai in the 1920s. While I was blissfully sipping this soup, Noel Coward may well have been writing his *Private Lives* in the Cathay Hotel up the road.

Method: Soak dried mushrooms in 300 mL (1 cup) of hot water for 30 minutes. Drain and remove stems. Cut each cap into 10 thin slices. Return the sliced dried mushrooms to the mushroom water to extract more flavour. Cut chicken into 2.5 x 1.5 cm (1 x ½ in) slices. Sprinkle with salt and dust with cornflour. Coat with egg white. Heat oil in a wok or frying pan. Stir-fry chicken in hot oil for 1 minute and drain. Remove the stems of the fresh mushrooms, wash thoroughly, and cut caps into 6 thin slices.

Add the dried mushrooms and mushroom water to a large pan containing the chicken stock. Bring contents to a gentle boil. Add ginger and pepper to taste. Simmer gently for 10 minutes. Add the fresh mushrooms, chicken and the soya sauce. Simmer gently for 10 minutes.

Serving: Pour the soup into individual bowls.

BASIC BEEF BROTH

Niu Rou Qing Tang

2 kg (4 lb) neck of beef or any
   stewing beef
4.2 L (4 quarts) cold water
3 slices root ginger
Salt to taste

4 portions

THIS BROTH IS USED as a base for such soups as Beef Broth and Spinach Soup with Beancurd.

Method: Cut beef into 2.5 cm (1 in) cubes. Place in 1.8 L (2 quarts) of cold water and refrigerate for 3 hours. Drain, then add the remaining quantity of water to the beef. Bring contents to the boil. Reduce heat and simmer for 2 hours, skimming every 30 minutes. Add the ginger and salt; simmer for 35 minutes. Strain. The broth can now be used in other dishes.

The beef cubes may be lightly sprinkled with soya sauce, chopped ginger and garlic and served with rice.

PAINTED SOUP

Hua Tang

2-3 egg whites
Shredded Pork and Sichuan Pickle
  Soup with Bean Thread
  Noodles (page 27)
Vegetable slices and skins, dried
  lily buds, herb leaves, etc., for
  "painting"

4-6 portions

WE CHINESE CAN no more paint on soup than walk on water! But we do garnish this soup with designs made from vegetables and other foods. To prepare a surface to paint or lay a design on, you simply beat egg whites until stiff. Fill a soup tureen two-thirds full of soup — Shredded Pork and Sichuan Pickle Soup with Bean Thread Noodles is ideal for this purpose — then, while it is still hot, spread the egg white thickly over the top. The egg white can be smoothed over with the side of a knife blade or a spatula. Once the egg white surface is smooth, any kind of design can be placed on it.

Chinese chefs often create tranquil rural scenes such as a fisherman dangling a fishing line through a hole in the egg white! They use yellow-brown golden needle (dried lily) buds for trunks of trees; thinly sliced green vegetables for foliage and leaves; cut discs of carrots for the sun; and tomato skins to make blazing red flowers. For a banquet, the more ambitious chef creates pictures of people and animals to further enliven the scene.

Serving: The soup should be warm when it is brought to the table. The host or hostess ladles part of the design and a portion of the soup into the individual bowls of the diners. Painted Soup will add fun to any dinner party.

BEEF BROTH AND SPINACH SOUP WITH BEANCURD

Bo Cai Doufu Tang

375 g (12 oz) young spinach
1 cake beancurd (tofu)
1.5 L (6 cups) Basic Beef Broth
  (page 22)
Salt to taste
Pepper to taste
2 slices root ginger
1½ tablespoons light soya sauce

4-5 portions

BECAUSE IT CONTAINS spinach and beancurd, this nourishing soup is appealing to health-conscious Westerners.

Method: Wash spinach thoroughly. Remove stems and cut leaves into 5 cm (2 in) wide horizontal slices. Cut beancurd into 2.5 cm (1 in) cubes. Bring beef broth to the boil in a large saucepan. Add the salt, pepper and ginger together with the spinach, beancurd and soya sauce. Simmer gently for 15 minutes.

Serving: Divide the contents evenly into soup bowls and serve.

WHOLE CHICKEN SOUP WITH CHINESE CABBAGE

Bai Cai Ji Tang

*1 chicken (approximately 2.25 kg/
    5-5½ lb)*
5-6 slices root ginger
2 medium onions, sliced
Salt to taste
Pepper to taste
2.2 L (4 pt) strong chicken stock
*1 medium Chinese (celery) cabbage
    (approximately 1-1.5 kg/2-3 lb)*
2 tablespoons light soya sauce
4-5 tablespoons rice wine or sherry

8-10 portions, with other dishes

THIS RICH AND LIGHT soup is a welcome addition to any multi-dish Chinese meal. It is usually cooked for at least 2½ hours in an earthenware pot placed inside a steamer. In the West it is best cooked in a large casserole in the oven.

Method: Rinse and dry the chicken inside and out and transfer breast up to a heatproof casserole. Add ginger and onion. Sprinkle the chicken with salt and pepper. Add stock and heat to boiling. Cover and transfer to an oven preheated to 200°C (400°F/Gas mark 6). Cook for 1¼ hours. Meanwhile, trim and wash the cabbage. Cut the cabbage into 10 lengthwise strips. Remove the casserole from the oven, turn the chicken over and place the cabbage strips under it. Pour the soya sauce and rice wine or sherry over the chicken. Return to the oven, reset the temperature to 180°C (360°F/Gas mark 4) and cook for 1¼ hours.

Serving: The dish should be served directly from the casserole. The chicken meat will be tender enough to be broken into pieces with a pair of chopsticks, then divided into the individual bowls of the diners. The cabbage can be served in the same manner.

SOUP OF THREE DELICIOUSNESS
San Xian Tang

*120-150 g (4-5 oz) boneless chicken
    breast*
Salt to taste
1 egg white, lightly beaten
1 tablespoon cornflour (cornstarch)
*1½ tablespoons dried prawns
    (shrimps)*
120-150 g (4-5 oz) asparagus
120 g (4 oz) canned bamboo shoots
5-6 fresh sea scallops, shelled
*5-6 king prawns (large shrimps),
    shelled and deveined*
*1.2 L (4½ cups) strong chicken
    stock*
2 slices root ginger
1½ tablespoons rice wine or sherry
Pepper to taste

4-5 portions

A LOT OF POETIC licence is used in Chinese culinary
expressions. Originally this soup contained only
three delicious ingredients — fresh prawns, fresh
scallops and bamboo shoots — but you may also
include dried prawns and asparagus. The main
concept, however, is that the soup should be lightly
cooked and the flavour should be a combination of
light, neutral and savoury tastes.

Method: Cut chicken into 4 x 2.5 cm (1½ x 1 in) thin
slices. Sprinkle with salt, dip in egg white, and dust
with cornflour. Poach in boiling water to cover for
1 minute, then drain. Boil with dried prawns in
600 mL (2⅔ cups) of water for 5 minutes and leave to
simmer gently a further 5 minutes, then drain.

   Cut asparagus and bamboo shoots slantwise into
1.5 cm (½ in) pieces. Cut the scallops and king
prawns into halves. Poach the seafood in boiling
water to cover for 1 minute, then drain.

   Heat stock in an earthenware or enamel pot.
Add chicken, dried prawns, ginger, bamboo shoots,
asparagus and rice wine or sherry. Bring to a gentle
boil and simmer for 5 minutes. Add king prawns and
scallops and continue simmering for 2½ minutes.
Adjust for seasoning and serve.

Serving: This is an excellent light soup to serve at a
party where many dishes are served during the
course of the meal.

SHREDDED PORK AND SICHUAN PICKLE SOUP WITH BEAN THREAD NOODLES

Zha Cai Rou Si Fen Si

4 medium dried black mushrooms
1½ tablespoons dried prawns
  (shrimps)
1.2 L (4¾ cups) chicken stock
90 g (3 oz) Sichuan pickles
120 g (4 oz) canned bamboo shoots
120 g (4 oz) lean pork
90 g (3 oz) bean thread
  (transparent) noodles
Salt to taste
Pepper to taste

4-6 portions

SICHUAN PICKLES ARE chilli-pickled mustard or cabbage. They have a very distinctive and spicy flavour and are often added to other foods to inject more zest. Here they are combined with shredded pork and bean thread noodles to produce one of the most frequently served soups in China.

Method: Soak dried mushrooms and dried prawns in 300 mL (1⅓ cups) hot water for 30 minutes. Drain, reserving the mushroom water. Remove and discard the stems of the mushrooms and cut caps into shreds. Add the shredded mushrooms, dried prawns and mushroom water to the chicken stock.

Rinse and wash the pickles under running water and cut into matchsticks. Cut bamboo shoots and pork into matchsticks. Soak noodles in hot water for 5 minutes, then drain and cut into 7.5 cm (3 in) length sections.

Bring the chicken stock and mushroom water to the boil in a large saucepan. Add pork, pickles and remaining ingredients. Simmer gently for 12-15 minutes. Serve.

Serving: The soup should be served in a large bowl for the diners to help themselves from a communal spoon. The soup is slightly spicy, so the diner may prefer to drink a mouthful a little at a time throughout the meal rather than all at once.

RICE AND NOODLES

RICE AND NOODLES

RICE is still the principal staple food eaten in China. Since the advent of the electric rice-cooker, the preparation of rice has become largely automatic yet it is still useful to know how to cook it in an ordinary saucepan. I often receive enquiries about how to cook rice, not infrequently from Chinese who have forgotton how to do it!

Next to rice, noodles are probably the most widely eaten staple food in China. Noodles are made from wheat flour, which is widely available in the north, as well as from rice flour, a product of the south and the Yangzi (Yangtze) River Valley.

There is some debate as to who actually invented noodles. One theory is that Marco Polo taught the Chinese how to make and use them. I believe that this is most unlikely, as flour was already being used to make noodles in China around the time of Julius Caesar, many centuries before Marco Polo! Besides, having gone through the *Memoirs of Marco Polo* with some care in the British Museum a few years ago, I never came across any mention of noodles at all, although there were lengthy descriptions of Chinese markets and eating establishments, which bettered anything he had seen in Europe. Furthermore, Chinese historical records state that the first recorded millionaires in Chinese history were flour merchants who lived during the pre-Christian eras of the Warring Kingdoms and the early Han Dynasty. These merchants very probably made their money by selling cakes and noodles! It seems most likely that the Italians and the Chinese made their own discoveries about pasta quite independently of each other, and over the centuries each country has developed its own tradition. The Italians use grated cheese and tomato for flavour and sauce, while the Chinese prepare and present their noodle dishes in the following ways:

• *Soup Noodles* (Tang Mian) — garnished noodles served in clear soups in bowls .
• *Braised or Pot-Cooked Noodles* (Hui Mian) — noodles pot-cooked in gravy or thickened sauce and served garnished in bowls.
• *Hot-Tossed or Cold-Tossed Noodles* (Ban Mian) — boiled noodles served tossed together in a savoury or aromatic sauce, often garnished with shredded meat and vegetables.
• *Stir-fried Noodles* (Chao Mian) — the best-known Chinese noodle dish in the West: noodles stir-fried with meat, seafood or vegetables and served on a plate rather than in a bowl. When the noodles are fried until crisp and brown, the dish is called Double Brown Noodles (Lian Wang Mian). The stir-fried ingredients are pushed to one side of the wok, more oil is added and the noodles are shallow-fried until crisp. The one drawback of this dish is that, like fried bread, it is sometimes too oily for contemporary taste!

BOILED RICE

Bai Fan

500 g (2½ cups) long-grain white rice
1 L (4 cups) water

4-6 portions

BOILED RICE should be fairly dry, as it is usually consumed with food served with ample sauce.

Method: Place rice in a saucepan. Rinse a couple of times and drain. Add water. Bring to the boil and cover with a tight-fitting lid. After 3-4 minutes, reduce the heat and simmer gently for 8-9 minutes. Turn the heat off completely and leave the rice to cook covered in its own steam for another 8-9 minutes. The rice will then be ready to serve.

BASIC FRIED RICE

Chao Fan

1-2 medium onions, chopped
2-3 tablespoons vegetable oil
2 eggs, beaten
500 g (2½ cups) boiled rice
Salt to taste

4-6 portions

FRIED RICE IS served more often in Chinese restaurants in the West than it is in China. Many Westerners are not used to eating plain boiled rice, which they may find tasteless or even insipid on its own. Basic Fried Rice is prepared by stir-frying beaten eggs and chopped onion with cooked rice (usually cold leftover rice from a previous meal). The fried onion provides aroma, the eggs richness, and the salt a touch of flavour.

Method: Stir-fry the onion for about 1½ minutes in the oil, then add the eggs. Once the eggs have set, add the rice and salt to taste. Stir until evenly mixed.

Serving: Serve with meat, fish, seafood, or vegetable dishes.

YANGZHOU FRIED RICE

Yangzhou Chao Fan

2-3 tablespoons vegetable oil
Chopped ham
Peeled cooked prawns (shrimps)
500 g (2½ cups) boiled rice
1-2 medium onions, chopped
Fresh or frozen peas
Diced cooked carrots
2 eggs, beaten
Salt to taste

4-6 portions

YANGZHOU IS A riverside town on the lower Yangzi (Yangtze) River. Here freshwater prawns (shrimps), crabs and fish, and all varieties of vegetables abound. The famous Jin Hua ham of this region is chopped along with peeled prawns stir-fried with boiled rice, and one or two vegetables such as peas to make Yangzhou Fried Rice or Superior Fried Rice. In restaurants this name applies to almost any fried rice to which several ingredients are added, such as diced chicken or beef. When these ingredients are stir-fried with onions, chopped ham, peas and diced carrots, the rice is so rich that it can be eaten on its own. However, out of sheer habit, the Chinese diner will still order a couple of savoury dishes to complement the rice. This is a useful dish to cook when you have a lot of leftover ingredients to use up. It can be a very tasty and substantial dish.

Method: There is no hard and fast rule for cooking Yangzhou Fried Rice. The main procedure is to stir-fry the chopped ingredients in quick sequence and toss them all together at the end.

CONGEE

Zhou

250-315 g (1¼-1½ cups) long-grain
or short-grain white rice
2.2-2.5 L (8-10 cups) water

4-6 portions

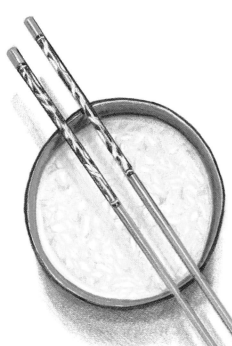

I WOULD CLASSIFY congee, or soft rice, as one of the most memorable dishes of China. It is served to the very young, the very old and the invalid.

One of the most digestible foods in the world, it is warm and settling to the stomach, and is served at breakfast and supper. On both occasions, bowls of congee are served with a selection of cold foods such as salt eggs, soya eggs, and 100-year-old eggs (1000-year-old eggs), as well as a variety of pickled vegetables, dried sausages and leftovers. Leftovers gain a new lease on life when eaten with this hot rice porridge, for the rice imparts a new dimension to dishes which could never be revived by simple reheating. Many Chinese look forward to congee for their early-morning breakfast as well as their midnight or "*après* mahjong" supper.

Method: Add the rice and the water to a heavy saucepan. Bring contents to the boil and immediately reduce heat. Simmer very gently, without covering, stirring every now and then so that no rice sticks to the bottom of the pan. After 1½ hours, test the rice to see if it is the right consistency (it should be like porridge). If it is getting too thick, add a little boiling water and continue to simmer, stirring every now and then, for 30 minutes until the rice is tender.

Serving: Congee is attractively presented in individual bowls for each diner.

SAVOURY SOFT RICE

Mei Wei Zhou

2.2 L (8 cups) chicken stock
250 g (1¼ cups) long-grain or
    short-grain white rice
1½ tablespoons dried prawns
    (shrimps)
1½ tablespoons light soya sauce
1 tablespoon finely chopped spring
    onions (scallions) or chives

4-6 portions

BASIC CONGEE CAN be transformed into Savoury Soft Rice simply by cooking the rice in chicken stock instead of water and adding dried prawns and soya sauce.

Method: Add the stock and the rice to a heavy saucepan. Bring contents to the boil, and immediately reduce the heat. Simmer gently, partially covered, and stir occasionally. Check the rice after 1½ hours. It should be the consistency of porridge. If it is too thick, add a little boiling water. Add the dried prawns and soya sauce and cook 30 minutes longer.

Serving: Garnish with finely chopped spring onions or chives just before serving.

HAINAN CHICKEN AND RICE

Hai Nan Ji Fan

*1 chicken weighing about 2.5 kg
   (4½-5 lb)*
500 g (1 lb) young leeks
2 medium onions, thinly sliced
3 L (12 cups) water
3 slices root ginger, shredded
Salt to taste
Pepper to taste
*500 g (2½ cups) long-grain white
   rice*

FOR THE SAUCE BOATS

*Soya sauce, vinegar, sesame oil,
   fresh chilli, root ginger, spring
   onion (scallion) and garlic
   (blend ingredients to taste)*

6-7 portions

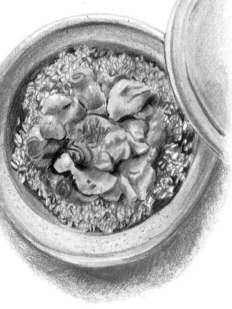

THIS SATISFYING DISH can be eaten on its own.

Method: Rinse and dry chicken inside and out. Chop
chicken through the bones into bite-size pieces. Clean
leeks thoroughly and cut slantwise into 4 cm (1½ in)
sections. Place the chicken pieces and onion in a large
wok or pot. Add water, ginger, salt and pepper to
taste. Bring contents to the boil and simmer gently
for 45 minutes. Pour three-quarters of the stock into
a saucepan and reserve.
   Rinse the rice and add it with leeks to the chicken
and remaining stock in the wok. Cover and bring
contents to a very gentle boil for 20 minutes.
Turn off heat. Allow the rice to absorb all the stock
and complete cooking in its own heat for 15 minutes.

Serving: Heat and season the reserved chicken stock.
When ready to serve, heat the wok or pot for about
1 minute, bring it to the dining table and open the lid
in a great cloud of steam. The wok or pot containing
the rice and chicken should be surrounded by an
array of small sauce bowls, each containing mixtures
of soya sauce, vinegar, sesame oil, chopped chilli,
ginger, spring onion and garlic, so diners can dip their
pieces of chicken in to give them additional zest.
Serve small bowls of the heated and seasoned
chicken stock alongside.

NOODLES TOSSED IN SESAME PASTE

Ma Jiang Ban Mian

500 g (1 lb) fresh wheat noodles
3 tablespoons light soya sauce
2 tablespoons rice wine vinegar
1½ tablespoons vegetable oil
3 spring onions (scallions), finely
chopped

SAUCE

2 tablespoons sesame paste or
peanut butter
1½ tablespoons vegetable oil
1 tablespoon sesame oil
1½ tablespoons chicken stock

3 portions

I AM INCLUDING this simple and inexpensive noodle recipe because it is so perennially appealing to such a wide number of people. I used to thoroughly enjoy tucking into a bowl of these nutty, aromatic noodles bought from a wayside stall on my way back from school in the 1920s.

Method: Place the noodles in a pan of boiling water and cook until tender (30 to 60 seconds for thin noodles, 2 to 4 minutes for thick noodles). Drain. Divide the noodles among as many bowls as there are people eating.
    To make the sauce, combine ingredients in a bowl until well blended.

Serving: Allow each diner to sprinkle an equal amount of soya sauce, vinegar, oil and spring onions over his or her own bowl of noodles. Top with sauce.

PEKING JA JIANG NOODLES

Beijing Zha Jiang Mian

500 g (1 lb) fresh wheat noodles
1 medium cucumber, cut into
matchsticks

SAUCE

4 tablespoons vegetable oil
250 g (½ lb) minced or ground raw
pork
1 medium onion, finely chopped
2 slices root ginger, finely chopped
2 cloves garlic, finely chopped
100 mL (½ cup) boiling water
2 tablespoons yellow bean sauce
2 tablespoons dark soya sauce
2 tablespoons tomato purée
3 tablespoons chicken stock
1 tablespoon cornflour (cornstarch)
blended with 4 tablespoons
water

4 portions

THIS DISH HAS a curious resemblance to Italian *pasta alla bolognese,* but it has shredded cucumber tossed in with the noodles and meat sauce, adding a crunchy texture to the dish. The use of soya sauce makes it more savoury than the Italian version.

Method: Place the noodles in a pan of boiling water and cook until tender (30 to 60 seconds for thin noodles, 2 to 4 minutes for thick noodles). Drain.

To make the sauce, heat the oil in a wok or large frying pan. When hot, add the pork, onion, ginger and garlic. Stir over medium heat for 3 minutes. Pour in boiling water. Raise heat to high. Bring contents to the boil. Add yellow bean sauce, soya sauce, tomato purée and stock. Stir while the sauce boils and reduces by half. Stir in the blended cornflour to thicken the sauce.

Serving: Place noodles in the middle of a large, well-heated serving plate and surround them with a circle of shredded cucumber. Pour the meat sauce on top of the noodles. Bring the dish to the dining table for the diners to toss the meat sauce and noodles together while still hot.

SHANGHAI COLD-TOSSED NOODLES
Shang Hai Leng Mian

2 tablespoons dried prawns
   (shrimps)
2 tablespoons rice wine or sherry
2 tablespoons rice wine vinegar
2 teaspoons chilli sauce
3 tablespoons light soya sauce
500 g (1 lb) fresh wheat noodles
2½ tablespoons Sichuan pickles,
   chopped
2 tablespoons green mustard
   pickles, chopped
2 tablespoons winter pickles,
   chopped
3 spring onions (scallions), cut
   diagonally into 1.5 cm (½ in)
   lengths
1 teaspoon sesame oil

4-5 portions

THIS IS ONE of the favourite dishes eaten during the hot summer in Shanghai.

Method: Soak the dried prawns in hot water for 10 minutes. Drain and chop them coarsely. Add rice wine or sherry to the chopped prawns to marinate briefly. Combine the vinegar, chilli sauce and soya sauce, and mix them well.

Cook the noodles in a pan of boiling water until tender (30 to 60 seconds for thin noodles, 2 to 4 minutes for thick noodles). Drain and cool.

Serving: Spread the noodles on a large serving plate. Sprinkle them evenly with coarsely chopped pickles, chopped prawns and rice wine or sherry, and then the soya sauce mixture. Add the spring onions and sesame oil.

To serve in the Chinese way, place the large serving plate at the centre of the table. Allow the diners to toss and mix the noodles with different ingredients according to individual preference.

BASIC SHREDDED PORK CHAO MIAN
Rou Si Chao Mian

*250-315 g (8-10 oz) fresh wheat
noodles*
*180 g (6 oz) pork belly (fresh bacon
or side pork)*
Salt to taste
Pepper to taste
3 spring onions (scallions)
60 g (2 oz) Sichuan pickles
3 tablespoons vegetable oil
2 slices root ginger, crushed
2 cloves garlic, crushed
120 g (4 oz) bean sprouts
2 tablespoons dark soya sauce
1½ tablespoons shrimp sauce
6 tablespoons chicken stock

2-3 portions

NOODLES ARE CONSUMED as snacks in China.
During a meal, they are eaten with rice and are
regarded as adding weight and substance.

Method: Boil the noodles in an ample amount of
water until tender (30 to 60 seconds for thin noodles,
2 to 4 minutes for thick noodles). Rinse under
running water to separate. Cut pork crosswise into
1 cm (⅓ in) matchsticks. Sprinkle with salt and
pepper. Cut spring onions into 1.5 cm (½ in) sections
and separate the green parts from the white.
Shred the pickles.
   Heat 2 tablespoons of oil in a wok or large frying
pan. When hot add the pork, ginger and garlic, the
whites of the spring onions and the shredded pickles.
Stir-fry them together over high heat for 2½ minutes.
Remove half the contents and reserve. Add half the
soya sauce, half the shrimp sauce and half the stock.
Bring contents to the boil. Add the noodles. Stir-fry
over medium heat for 2 minutes. Transfer the
contents to a large serving dish.
   Heat the remaining tablespoon of oil. When hot,
return the reserved mixture to the pan. Stir-fry over
high heat for 1½ minutes, adding bean sprouts, the
remaining soya sauce, shrimp sauce and stock, and
the greens of the spring onions. Stir-fry for 45
seconds over high heat.

Serving: Remove all the ingredients from the pan and
place them on top of the noodles piled up on the
serving plate. Serve with extra shredded pickle.

BRAISED BIRTHDAY NOODLES WITH RED-COOKED PORK

Hong Shao Zhu Rou Shou Mian

500 g (1 lb) pork belly (fresh bacon or side pork)
2 cloves garlic, chopped
2 slices root ginger, chopped
2 teaspoons sugar
3 tablespoons rice wine or sherry
5 tablespoons dark soya sauce
300 mL (1⅓ cups) water
300 mL (1⅓ cups) chicken stock
1 tablespoon cornflour (cornstarch) blended with 4 tablespoons water
180 g (6 oz) French beans (green beans)
250 g (8 oz) fresh thick wheat noodles or egg noodles
2 soya eggs or hard-boiled eggs

4 portions

IN CHINA, THE EGG symbolises continuity and fertility so it is frequently included in birthday dishes. In this dish, the top of each bowl of noodles is decorated with half a hard-boiled egg or soya egg (an egg which has been hard-boiled in soya sauce).

Method: To prepare the red-cooked pork, cut the pork crosswise, into 5 x 2.5 cm (2 x 1 in) thin pieces. Cook the pork pieces in a wok or frying pan with garlic, ginger, sugar and rice wine or sherry for 3 minutes. Add the soya sauce and water, and simmer over very low heat for 1 hour. Add stock and simmer for a further 15 minutes. Stir in the blended cornflour to thicken the sauce.

Wash and trim the beans. Place the noodles and beans in a heavy pot or heatproof casserole. Pour the pork and gravy over the noodles and beans. Simmer gently for 2 to 4 minutes or until tender.

Serving: Divide the noodles and sauce among 4 large bowls. Decorate by topping each with half a soya egg or hard-boiled egg.

LAMB AND LEEK MANCHURIAN BRAISED NOODLES

Man Zhou Da Suan Yang Rou Mian

875 g (1¾ lb) leg of lamb
Salt to taste
Pepper to taste
Cornflour (cornstarch) for
    dredging
375 g (¾ lb) young leeks
4 tablespoons vegetable oil
3 slices root ginger, shredded
3 cloves garlic, crushed
900 mL (4 cups) strong chicken
    stock
3 tablespoons light soya sauce
4 tablespoons rice wine or sherry
375 g (12 oz) fresh wheat noodles
½ teaspoon sesame oil

4-5 portions

CONSUMING THIS SOUP is a very warming experience!

Method: Cut the lamb into bite-size 4 cm (1½ in) cubes. Sprinkle with salt and pepper and dredge in cornflour. Clean leeks thoroughly and cut diagonally into 5 cm (2 in) sections.

Heat oil in a heavy saucepan. When hot, add ginger, garlic and lamb. Stir-fry for 5 minutes. Add 600 mL (2⅔ cups) stock and bring to the boil. Reduce heat to low and simmer gently for 1 hour.

Add the leeks and the remaining stock to the stew. Bring to the boil again. Simmer gently together for 5 minutes. Add the soya sauce and rice wine or sherry. Add noodles and cook until tender (30 to 60 seconds for thin noodles, 2 to 4 minutes for thick noodles). Sprinkle lightly with sesame oil and serve.

Serving: Divide the noodles, lamb and leeks among the diners' bowls and serve everyone with chopsticks (rather than spoons), as they are supposed to drink the broth directly from the bowls.

TEN TREASURE BRAISED BEAN THREAD NOODLES

Shi Jin Fen Si

4 medium black dried mushrooms
90 g (3 oz) pork
90 g (3 oz) boneless chicken breasts
120 g (4 oz) celery
60 g (2 oz) canned bamboo shoots
2 spring onions (scallions)
90 g (3 oz) French beans (green beans)
1 small red capsicum (bell pepper)
185 g (6 oz) bean thread (transparent) noodles
1½ tablespoons dried prawns (shrimps)
5 tablespoons vegetable oil
2 slices bacon, cut into matchsticks
1 medium onion, thinly sliced
2 slices root ginger, chopped
2 cloves garlic, chopped
300 mL (1⅓ cups) strong chicken stock
2 tablespoons dark soya sauce
3 tablespoons rice wine or sherry
Dash sesame oil

6-10 portions

THIS IS ONE of the favourite dishes in the Liberation Army. Simply called the Big Pot Dish (Da Huo Cai), it makes a spartan army meal of plain rice more palatable!

Method: Soak dried mushrooms in 150 mL (⅔ cup) hot water for 30 minutes. Drain, reserving mushroom water. Cut caps into shreds, discarding stems. Cut pork, chicken, celery, bamboo shoots, spring onions, French beans and red capsicum into matchsticks. Immerse noodles in hot water for 15 minutes, cut into 10 cm (4 in) sections and drain thoroughly. Soak dried prawns in hot water for 15 minutes. Drain and chop finely.

Heat 3 tablespoons of oil in a saucepan. When hot, add the prawns, dried mushrooms, bacon and onion. Stir-fry them together over medium heat for 5 minutes. Pour in the mushroom water. Bring contents to the boil. Add the bean thread noodles and stir them through. Set aside.

Heat remaining 1 tablespoon of oil in a saucepan. When hot, add ginger, garlic, celery, bamboo shoots, spring onions, shredded pork and chicken, and stir-fry over medium heat for 4-5 minutes. Add beans, capsicum, stock, and pour in the soya sauce and rice wine or sherry. Cook gently together for 5 minutes.

Add the contents of the first pan to the second pan. Mix together and heat through for 5 minutes, or until noodles are tender.

Serving: Top with a dash of sesame oil and serve.

CANTONESE RICE NOODLES WITH BEEF IN BLACK BEAN SAUCE

Chi Zhi Niu He

*375 g (12 oz) fresh or dried rice
    flour noodles*
3 spring onions (scallions)
*500 g (1 lb) lean beef steak, such as
    rump, fillet or topside (sirloin)*
Salt to taste
1 egg white, lightly beaten
*1½ tablespoons cornflour
    (cornstarch)*
1 red capsicum (bell pepper)
4 tablespoons vegetable oil
2 medium onions, thinly sliced
2 slices root ginger, shredded
2 cloves garlic, crushed

SAUCE

*2 tablespoons salted black beans,
    soaked in hot water for
    3 minutes, then chopped*
*1¼ tablespoons cornflour
    (cornstarch) blended with
    4 tablespoons water*
2 tablespoons dark soya sauce
1½ tablespoons oyster sauce
1 tablespoon chilli sauce
4 tablespoons beef stock

4-5 portions

HE FEN NOODLES ARE flat, ribbonlike rice flour noodles which are generally sold freshly made. The attraction of this dish lies principally in its beefy flavour and the spicy and earthy black beans.

Method: Soak dried noodles in hot water until tender. Fresh noodles do not need soaking. Drain and rinse under running water to separate. Cut spring onions diagonally into 5 cm (2 in) sections. Cut beef into 4 x 1.5 cm (1½ x ½ in) strips. Sprinkle with salt, dip in egg white and dust with cornflour. Seed capsicum and cut it into thin strips.

Heat oil in a wok or large frying pan. When hot add the onions, ginger and garlic; stir-fry for 1½ minutes and push them to one side of the pan. Add beef to the centre of the wok and cook 1 minute; push beef aside. To make the sauce, add oil to pan; heat and stir in chopped black beans. Thicken the sauce by stirring in the blended cornflour. Bring the beef, onions, ginger and garlic back to the mix and stir in the remaining sauce ingredients. Cook together for 1 minute. Remove half the beef and sauce from the pan, cover and set aside. Add the noodles to the remaining beef and sauce mixture. Stir together over medium heat for 1½ minutes.

Serving: Transfer the contents of the pan onto a large serving plate. Add the spring onions and capsicum to the pan together with the beef and sauce which has been put aside. Stir-fry for 30 seconds over high heat. Pour over beef on the serving plate to garnish.

SINGAPORE RICE-STICK NOODLES

Xing Zhou Chao Mi

375 g (12 oz) rice-stick noodles
3 tablespoons dried prawns
   (shrimps)
180 g (6 oz) barbecued pork
2 spring onions (scallions), cut
   diagonally
3 tablespoons vegetable oil
2 small onions, thinly sliced
2 slices bacon, cut into matchsticks
Salt to taste
2½ tablespoons curry powder or to
   taste
5 tablespoons chicken stock
90 g (3 oz) cooked prawns
   (shrimps), peeled and deveined
1½ tablespoons light soya sauce
180 g (6 oz) bean sprouts

4-5 portions

THIS IS NOT the most refined of Chinese dishes, but it is very popular and often appears on the menus of Chinese restaurants abroad. The mild curry flavour gives the dish a South Sea character and zest.

Method: Soak noodles in hot water for 20 minutes, or until tender; drain thoroughly. Soak dried prawns in a small bowl of hot water for 15 minutes. Drain and chop roughly. Cut barbecued pork into 5 x 2.5 cm (2 x 1 in) slices and spring onions into 4 cm (1½ in) sections.
   Heat 2 tablespoons of oil in a wok or frying pan. When hot, add onions, soaked prawns and bacon, and stir-fry over medium heat for 1½ minutes. Add salt and 2 tablespoons curry powder, and stir-fry 1 more minute. Add stock and stir to form a bubbling sauce. Add the noodles and stir to coat with the sauce.
   Heat remaining 1 tablespoon oil in a separate wok or pan. When hot, add the cooked prawns, sliced barbecued pork, soya sauce and the remaining ½ tablespoon of curry powder. Stir-fry for about a minute. Add the bean sprouts and spring onions, turn the heat up high and stir-fry all the ingredients together for just over a minute.

Serving: Combine the contents of the two woks, stir a few times and serve on one large serving plate.

HOT-TOSSED NOODLES WITH ASPARAGUS

Lu Sun Ban Mian

250-315 g (8-10 oz) fresh wheat
 noodles
185 g (6 oz) asparagus
150 mL (⅔ cup) strong chicken
 stock
2 tablespoons vegetable oil
2 cloves garlic, chopped
1½ tablespoons light soya sauce

4-5 portions

SURPRISINGLY, THE COMBINATION of fresh crunchy asparagus and soft noodles in this dish appeals to people who are normally big meat-eaters!

Method: Boil the noodles until tender (30–60 seconds for thin noodles, 2-4 minutes for thick noodles); drain. Remove 2.5 cm (1 in) of the root end of the asparagus and cut diagonally into 5 cm (2 in) sections. Heat stock in a small saucepan. Add the asparagus to simmer in the stock for 2-3 minutes. Turn asparagus several times so it will cook evenly. Heat the oil in a wok or frying pan and add the garlic. Stir-fry over medium heat for about 1 minute, then add the asparagus, stock and the noodles and mix them for a couple of minutes.

Serving: Transfer the noodles and asparagus to a large serving plate. Sprinkle with soya sauce and serve hot. Allow the diners themselves to do the final tossing together of the noodles and asparagus on their own plates.

THREE-MUSHROOM NOODLES

San Dong Mian

*10 medium or large dried black
    mushrooms*
*10 medium or large fresh
    mushrooms*
*180 g (6 oz) canned Chinese straw
    mushrooms*
250 g (8 oz) dried wheat noodles
3 tablespoons vegetable oil
*2 spring onions (scallions), finely
    chopped*
2 cloves garlic, crushed
*120-180 g (4-6 oz) canned braised
    bamboo shoots, cut into
    matchsticks*
2 tablespoons light soya sauce

3-4 portions

THIS DISH IS HEAVEN for mushroom lovers.

Method: Soak the dried mushrooms in a bowl of hot water for 30 minutes; drain, reserving half the water. Remove and discard the stems and cut caps into quarters. Clean and cut the caps of fresh mushrooms into quarters, also discarding the stems. Drain the straw mushrooms, retaining half the water from the can and add the water used for soaking the dried mushrooms. Heat them together in a saucepan to reduce liquid to half its original volume. Remove from heat.

Boil the noodles for 4-5 minutes, or until half cooked. Drain completely, and add them to soak in the reduced mushroom water to absorb the mushroom flavour.

Heat 2 tablespoons of oil in a frying pan. When hot add half the spring onions and garlic, and stir-fry them with the quartered dried mushrooms for 2 minutes. Add half the fresh mushrooms, bamboo shoots, 1 tablespoon soya sauce and the straw mushrooms and the reserved mushroom water; stir-fry them all together for 3 minutes.

Add the noodles to the other ingredients in the pan. Allow them to cook gently together for 3-4 minutes or until tender. Transfer the contents of the pan onto a large serving plate.

Heat remaining 1 tablespoon oil in a wok or frying pan. When hot, add the remaining garlic, spring onions, bamboo shoots, soya sauce and mushrooms. Stir-fry them over high heat for 2½ minutes.

Serving: Place the mushrooms and bamboo shoots as a garnish on top of the noodles on the serving plate.

DOUBLE-CRISP NOODLES WITH BEEF AND SEAFOOD
Hai Xian Niu Rou Chao Mian

250 g (8 oz) fresh wheat noodles
150 mL (⅔ cup) vegetable oil

TOPPING AND SAUCE

180 g (6 oz) lean beef steak, such as
  fillet, rump, topside (sirloin)
120 g (4 oz) shelled prawns
  (shrimps)
Salt to taste
1 egg white, lightly beaten
1½ tablespoons cornflour
  (cornstarch)
2 spring onions (scallions), finely
  chopped
2 slices root ginger, shredded
2 cloves garlic, finely chopped
2½ tablespoons dark soya sauce
1½ tablespoons oyster sauce
4 tablespoons beef stock
1 tablespoon cornflour (cornstarch)
  blended with 4 tablespoons
  water

4 portions

SOME PEOPLE IN CHINA enjoy noodles which are partially crispy. Diners will find the noodles in this dish crispy on the outside but still soft on the inside. When this is allied to the topping it adds a new dimension to the whole dish.

Method: Add the noodles to a pan of boiling water and cook thin noodles 30–60 seconds and thick noodles 2–4 minutes, or until tender. Drain thoroughly and heat oil in a wok or frying pan. When hot (a crumb will sizzle when dropped into it) add the noodles in a mass. Press them down to fry over high heat for 3-3½ minutes on each side, or until both sides are slightly brown and crispy. Leaving a small amount of oil for stir-frying the toppings, drain the noodles and transfer them to a serving plate.

Prepare the beef by cutting it into 5 x 2.5 cm (2 x 1 in) thin slices. Sprinkle the beef and the prawns with salt, dip them in egg white and dust with cornflour.

Heat the oil remaining in the wok or frying pan. When hot, add the beef, prawns, spring onions, ginger and garlic. Stir-fry them over high heat for 2 minutes. Add the soya sauce, oyster sauce and stock. Stir-fry over high heat for 1 minute. Add blended cornflour to the pan to thicken the bubbling sauce and stir in well.

Serving: Pour the sauce in the wok or pan over the noodles on the serving plate.

VEGETABLES, BEANCURD AND EGGS

VEGETABLES, BEANCURD AND EGGS

THE CHINESE EAT A large number of vegetable-based dishes along with rice and noodles.

Three of the most popular Chinese vegetable dishes — *Kai Yang Bai Cai, Chao Bo Cai* and *Hong Shao Bai Cai* — are included here.

While many of the dishes included in this book feature meat, most Chinese eat very small amounts of meat and dairy foods, so to obtain protein they eat beancurd (tofu) and eggs.

Reputed to be richer in protein than most meats, beancurd is cheaper and more easily digested. It is becoming increasingly popular in the health-conscious West.

Beancurd is derived from soya bean purée which has been boiled in water and then clarified and filtered for its milk. The milk is set overnight by cooking. When set, beancurd has the texture of a firm custard. It is normally sold as cakes 7.5 x 7.5 cm (3 x 3 in) and about 2.5 cm (1 in) thick, which can be cut into any shape or size.

Beancurd's neutral taste makes it ideal for Chinese cooking, as it readily absorbs the flavours of the food it is cooked with. Because it is so versatile, it is a great boon to vegetarians.

There is an abundance of poultry in China and egg dishes are extremely popular because they are easily prepared and versatile. Eggs are usually stir-fried (with one, two, or more ingredients added), but they also may be steamed in savoury custards (which are excellent to eat with plain boiled rice). The majority of Chinese egg dishes are comparatively basic, and they are a mainstay of the

Chinese diet. Beaten eggs are ideal to mix with meat, seafood and vegetables. This produces highly palatable dishes, which can be prepared in a minimal length of time.

STIR-FRIED CHINESE CABBAGE

Kai Yang Bai Cai

1 medium Chinese (celery) cabbage
   (about 500 g/1 lb)
2-2½ tablespoons dried prawns
   (shrimps)
3 tablespoons vegetable oil
2 slices root ginger, shredded
Salt to taste
1½ tablespoons light soya sauce

5-6 portions with other dishes

THIS IS ONE of the most common vegetable dishes on the Chinese dining table.

Method: Clean and cut cabbage into 5 cm (2 in) slices. Soak prawns in hot water for 10 minutes and drain.
   Heat oil in a saucepan. When hot, add ginger and dried prawns and stir over medium heat for 1½ minutes. Add the cabbage, sprinkle with salt and stir for 1½ minutes. Add the soya sauce and stir-fry for another 1½ minutes.

Serving: The dish should be served with other savoury dishes.

STIR-FRIED SPINACH
Chao Bo Cai

500 g (1 lb) fresh spinach
3 tablespoons vegetable oil
4-5 cloves garlic, crushed
Salt to taste
2 spring onions (scallions), diced
1½ teaspoons fermented beancurd
   (tofu) optional
1 tablespoon light soya sauce

4-5 portions with other dishes

THIS IS EXCELLENT to serve with all meat and poultry dishes.

Method: Stem the spinach and wash well. Cut into 5-8 cm (2-3 in) slices.
   Heat oil in a wok or large frying pan. Add garlic, salt and spring onions. Stir-fry for 30 seconds. Add the beancurd. Mash in the oil over medium heat. Add the spinach. Mix everything together well. Sprinkle evenly with soya sauce and cook gently for 1½ minutes. Stir once more.

Serving: Serve on a well-heated plate.

RED-COOKED CHINESE CABBAGE

Hong Shao Bai Cai

1 medium Chinese (celery)
  cabbage, weighing about 700 g
  (1½ lb)
1½ tablespoons dried prawns
  (shrimps)
2 tablespoons vegetable oil
2 slices root ginger, shredded
2 cloves garlic, crushed
Salt to taste
400 mL (1¾ cups) strong chicken
  stock
4½ tablespoons dark soya sauce
2 teaspoons sugar

5-6 portions with other dishes

CONSUME THIS SUMPTUOUS DISH with quantities of
plain boiled rice.

Method: Clean and cut cabbage into 5 x 8 cm
(2 x 3 in) slices. Soak dried prawns in hot water for
5 minutes and drain.
  Heat oil in large saucepan. When hot add the
ginger and garlic. Stir them over medium heat for
30 seconds. Add the cabbage, prawns and salt,
mixing in well. Pour in the stock and bring contents
to the boil. Reduce heat to low, add soya sauce and
sugar. Cover and cook gently for 10-12 minutes,
stirring occasionally.

Serving: This dish has lots of gravy, so it should be
served in a large bowl rather than a flat serving
plate.

RED-COOKED EGGPLANT

Hong Shao Qie Zi

2 medium Italian eggplants
  (aubergines)
1½ tablespoons dried prawns
  (shrimps)
3 tablespoons vegetable oil
Salt to taste
2 slices root ginger, shredded
3 cloves garlic, crushed
1 fresh green chilli, seeded and
  chopped
1 dried red chilli, seeded and
  chopped
3 tablespoons dark soya sauce
3 tablespoons chicken stock
2 tablespoons rice wine or sherry

5-6 portions with other dishes

THIS IS A very rich vegetable dish.

Method: Cut the eggplant into thin slices (1.5 cm or
½ in). Soak dried prawns in hot water for
10 minutes, then drain and chop coarsely.

   Heat oil in a wok or frying pan. When hot, add the
chopped dried prawns, salt, ginger, garlic and the
chillies. Stir over medium heat for about a minute.
Add the soya sauce and stock. Stir until the sauce
bubbles. Add all the eggplant and stir to coat with
sauce. Reduce heat to low and cook slowly for
4-5 minutes. Add the rice wine or sherry and stir.
Cook 3 more minutes and serve.

STIR-FRIED ASPARAGUS WITH GARLIC
Suan Zi Lu Sun

500 g (1 lb) young asparagus
3½ tablespoons vegetable oil
2 cloves garlic, crushed
1½ teaspoons sugar
1 tablespoon light soya sauce, or to taste
3 tablespoons chicken or vegetable stock
1 tablespoon Hoisin sauce, or to taste
1 tablespoon shrimp sauce, or to taste
1 tablespoon cornflour (cornstarch) blended with 3 tablespoons water

4-5 portions with other dishes

THE RICH SAUCE and the asparagus combine to make this a very tasty stir-fry. Use less soya sauce, Hoisin sauce and shrimp sauce for a milder, less salty dish.

Method: Remove and discard the root ends of the asparagus. Cut each spear diagonally into approximately 5 cm (2 in) sections.

Heat oil in a wok or frying pan. When hot add garlic and asparagus. Stir over medium heat for 2 minutes. Add the sugar, soya sauce, stock, shrimp sauce and Hoisin sauce. Stir contents over medium heat for 45 seconds. Reduce heat and continue to cook 1½ minutes. Add the blended cornflour and stir the mixture a few more times.

PUMPKIN STEW WITH TOMATOES, PEAS AND POTATOES

Shi Jin Dong Gua Tang

1.25 kg (2½ lbs) Japanese (kabocha) pumpkin (nam gwa)
500 g (1 lb) potatoes
4 medium tomatoes
1¼ tablespoons dried prawns (shrimps)
3 tablespoons vegetable oil
1 medium onion, thinly sliced
2 slices bacon, cut into matchsticks
2 slices root ginger, shredded
2 cloves garlic, crushed
600 mL (2⅔ cups) chicken stock
2 teaspoons sugar
3 tablespoons light soya sauce
Salt to taste
Pepper to taste
250 g (1 cup) green peas

10 portions with other dishes

THIS THICK SOUP is suitable for 10 diners when served with other dishes.

Method: Cut a large circle in the top of the shell and scoop out the flesh with a large spoon. Reserve the shell for use as a serving bowl. Dice squash flesh into 2 cm (¾ in) cubes. Peel and dice potatoes into similar cubes. Skin the tomatoes and cut into quarters. Soak dried prawns in hot water for 10 minutes, then drain and chop coarsely.

Heat oil in a large saucepan. When hot, add onion, bacon, ginger, garlic, and dried prawns. Stir-fry over medium heat for a couple of minutes. Add the diced squash and potato cubes, and stir over medium heat for 5 minutes. Pour in the stock, sugar and soya sauce, and season with salt and pepper to taste. Add the peas and the tomatoes. Bring contents to boil, reduce heat and simmer gently for 20 minutes.

Serving: A favourite way of serving this dish is in the hollow pumpkin shell. Place the shell in a large heatproof bowl. Pour the stew from the saucepan into the pumpkin. Place the pumpkin shell in a steamer and steam for 5-6 minutes. Bring it steaming and piping hot to the dining table for the diners to help themselves.

MIXED SPRING VEGETABLE STEW WITH BEAN THREAD NOODLES

Ji Cai Fen Si

*1½ tablespoons dried prawns
   (shrimps)*
3 young carrots
1 medium cucumber
2 spring onions (scallions)
250 g (8 oz) spinach
1 lettuce
*120 g (4 oz) bean thread
   (transparent) noodles*
4 tablespoons vegetable oil
2 slices bacon, cut into matchsticks
2 medium onions, thinly sliced
2 slices root ginger, shredded
2 cloves garlic, chopped
*250 g (8 oz) French beans (green
   beans), trimmed and halved*
250 g (8 oz) broccoli florets
600 mL (2⅔ cups) chicken stock
250 g (8 oz) bean sprouts
4-5 medium tomatoes, quartered
2 tablespoons light soya sauce
1½ tablespoons shrimp sauce
2 teaspoons sesame oil
Salt and pepper to taste

7-8 portions with other dishes

IN THE CONTEXT of a Chinese meal, this dish should be treated like a hot salad and consumed with both meat and rice.

Method: Soak dried prawns in hot water for 10 minutes, drain and chop coarsely. Cut carrots and cucumber diagonally into 5 cm (2 in) sections, spring onions into 1.5 cm (½ in) sections, spinach and lettuce into 5 cm (2 in) slices; soak noodles in hot water for 15 minutes, then cut into 8-10 cm (3-4 in) sections.

Heat vegetable oil in a large saucepan. When hot, add dried prawns, bacon, onions, ginger, garlic and carrots and stir-fry for 2 minutes. Add beans, broccoli and cucumber and continue to stir-fry over medium heat for 2 minutes. Pour in the stock and add the bean sprouts, spinach, tomatoes and lettuce. Bring contents to a gentle boil, add soya sauce and shrimp sauce and simmer gently for 15 minutes. Add the noodles, stirring to coat with sauce. Add spring onions and sesame oil, and simmer stew gently for 6-7 minutes or until noodles are tender. Add salt and pepper to taste and serve.

Serving: Because this is a stew, serve in a large bowl rather than on a flat serving plate.

STIR-FRIED BEAN SPROUTS WITH SICHUAN PICKLES AND SHREDDED PORK

Zha Cai Dou Ya Rou Si

500 g (1 lb) bean sprouts
2 spring onions (scallions)
3 tablespoons vegetable oil
120 g (4 oz) pork belly (fresh bacon
*   or side pork), cut into*
*   matchsticks*
60 g (2 oz) Sichuan pickles, cut
*   into matchsticks*
1½ tablespoons dark soya sauce
1 tablespoon rice wine vinegar
1½ teaspoons sesame oil
Salt to taste
Pepper to taste

4-5 portions with other dishes

IT IS COMMON in Chinese vegetable cooking, especially when stir-frying, to incorporate meat or seafood to enhance the flavour of the dish.

Method: Wash and dry the bean sprouts. Cut spring onions diagonally into 2.5 cm (1 in) sections.

Heat vegetable oil in a wok or frying pan. When hot, add pork and pickles and stir-fry over high heat for 1½ minutes. Add spring onions and stir-fry for 30 seconds. Add the bean sprouts and stir-fry for 1½ minutes. Sprinkle mixture with soya sauce, vinegar and sesame oil. Stir-fry over high heat for 1 minute. Season to taste with salt and pepper.

Serving: Serve hot on a well-heated plate. This dish should be accompanied by boiled rice and other savoury dishes.

BUDDHISTS' DELIGHT, OR FOOD FOR THE MINOR GODS

Luo Han Zhai

DRIED INGREDIENTS

6 medium dried black mushrooms
4 tablespoons wood ear fungus
4 tablespoons dried hair vegetable
4 tablespoons dried bamboo shoots
3 dried lily buds
7 g (½ oz) dried chestnuts
2 dried beancurd (tofu) sticks
120-150 g (4-5 oz) bean thread
     (transparent) noodles
3½ tablespoons vegetable oil
4 tablespoons lotus nuts
4 slices dried gingko nuts
Salt to taste
Pepper to taste

FRESH INGREDIENTS

2 sticks celery cut into 5 cm (2 in)
     sections and shredded
75 g (2½ oz) fresh mushrooms
2 spring onions (scallions), cut into
     5 cm (2 in) sections
4 large Chinese (celery) cabbage
     leaves
60 g (2 oz) cauliflower florets
75 g (2½ oz) broccoli florets
1 green capsicum (bell pepper),
     seeded and cut into 1.5 cm
     (½ in) strips
Salt to taste
3 tablespoons vegetable oil
2 teaspoons sesame oil

THE LUO HANS ARE minor gods whose images line the side walls of the monasteries and temples in China by the hundreds. This dish was created to feed them. It is prepared by stewing dried vegetables, fresh vegetables and bean thread noodles in a seasoned vegetable stock.

To serve, a very large bowl was placed at the centre of the monastery table for the monks, and presumably also the Luo Hans, to gather around and consume with chopsticks.

Method: Soak the dried mushrooms in hot water for 30 minutes, then drain. Remove and discard stems and cut caps into quarters. Rinse and clean wood ear fungus in warm water. Rinse and soak hair vegetable for 5 minutes and drain. Rinse dried bamboo shoots, soak for 15 minutes and cut into 5 cm (2 in) sections. Soak dried lily buds for 5 minutes in water and cut into 5 cm (2 in) sections. Soak dried chestnuts in hot water for 1 hour and cut into halves. Break tofu sticks into 5 cm (2 in) sections, soak in hot water for 25 minutes and drain. Soak noodles in hot water for 15 minutes; drain and cut into 8 cm (3 in) sections.

Cook all the dried ingredients, except for the bean thread noodles, and the fresh ingredients separately by stir-frying them for 3-4 minutes over medium heat in 1½ tablespoons hot oil in two woks or saucepans. Stir-fry them for 3-4 minutes each over medium heat. Finally combine the two lots of cooked foods into one large wok or pan.

SAUCE

*600 mL (2⅔ cups) strong vegetable
   stock*
3 tablespoons light soya sauce
*1½ tablespoons fermented
   beancurd (tofu)*
3 tablespoons rice wine or sherry

6-8 portions

To make the sauce, add the stock, soya sauce,
beancurd, and rice wine or sherry to the pan. Bring
contents to a gentle boil. Add the noodles. Stir and
turn to mix evenly with other ingredients in the pan.
Continue to stir and simmer until the noodles are
tender.

Serving: This dish should be served in a large
communal bowl placed at the centre of the table for
the diners to help themselves.

STIR-FRY OF DRIED AND FRESH MUSHROOMS
Chao Shuang Dong

10 medium dried black
   mushrooms
12 large fresh mushrooms
3½ tablespoons vegetable oil
4 tablespoons chicken stock
1½ tablespoons light soya sauce
1 tablespoon shrimp sauce
1 tablespoon cornflour (cornstarch)
   blended with 4 tablespoons
   water

4-5 portions with other dishes

THIS UNIQUELY FLAVOURED DISH will appeal to all mushroom lovers.

Method: Soak dried mushrooms in hot water for 30 minutes. Drain. Remove the stems of both the dried and the fresh mushrooms.
   Heat oil in a wok or frying pan. When hot, add the dried mushrooms to shallow-fry over low heat, stem side down, for 3 minutes. Add the fresh mushrooms, placing them stem side down, and cook 3 minutes. Add the stock, soya sauce, and shrimp sauce. Stir and mix the sauces with the mushrooms for 1 minute. Add the blended cornflour, pouring it evenly over the contents. Stir-fry gently for 1½ minutes.

Serving: An attractive way to serve this dish is to decorate the edge of the serving plate with some of the fresh mushroom caps facing downwards. There is a singularly distinct flavour to this dish.

STIR-FRIED GREEN PEAS WITH DRIED AND FRESH PRAWNS

Qing Dou Ha Ren

*1½ tablespoons dried prawns
(shrimps)*
1 spring onion (scallion)
2½ tablespoons vegetable oil
2 slices root ginger, shredded
2 cloves garlic, crushed
*4 tablespoons fresh or frozen baby
prawns (shrimps), shelled*
3 tablespoons chicken stock
375 g (12 oz) fresh or frozen peas
1½ tablespoons light soya sauce
1 tablespoon shrimp sauce
1½ teaspoons sesame oil
Salt to taste
Pepper to taste

5-6 portions with other dishes

THIS POPULAR DISH is quick to prepare, easy to cook and refreshingly different.

Method: Soak dried prawns in hot water for 10 minutes. Drain and chop coarsely. Diagonally cut spring onion into 2.5 cm (1 in) sections.

Heat the vegetable oil in a wok or frying pan. When hot, add dried prawns, ginger and garlic. Stir over medium heat for 30 seconds. Add fresh prawns, spring onion and stock. When contents come to the boil, stir for 15 seconds. Add the peas, soya sauce, shrimp sauce and sesame oil. Stir and turn gently until peas are tender. Season to taste with salt and pepper. Serve.

Serving: This attractive and colourful dish can be served with any combination of other savoury dishes and rice.

COLD-TOSSED BEANCURD WITH SICHUAN PICKLES AND DRIED PRAWNS

Ha Mi Zha Cai Ban Doufu

SAUCE

*3 tablespoons dried prawns
(shrimps)*
*2 tablespoons Sichuan pickles,
coarsely chopped*
*1½ tablespoons green mustard
pickles, coarsely chopped*
2 cloves garlic, finely chopped
2 teaspoons sugar
2½ tablespoons rice wine or sherry
2½ tablespoons dark soya sauce
*2½ tablespoons fresh lemon juice or
rice wine vinegar*
2½ tablespoons vegetable oil
½ tablespoon sesame oil

3 cakes beancurd (tofu)

5-6 portions as hors d'oeuvre

SERVE AS AN hors d'oeuvre or with plain boiled rice.

Method: To make the sauce, soak the dried prawns in hot water for 10 minutes; drain and finely chop. Combine chopped Sichuan pickles, green mustard pickles, garlic and chopped dried prawns in a bowl. Add sugar, wine, soya sauce, lemon juice or vinegar, vegetable and sesame oils. Mix them well together. Cut the beancurd into 1.5 cm (½ in) cubes.

Serving: Pile beancurd cubes on a serving plate. Spoon the sauce over the beancurd and toss them lightly together.

STIR-FRIED BEANCURD WITH MUSHROOMS AND SPRING ONIONS
Dong Gu Doufu

4 cakes beancurd (tofu)
8 medium fresh mushrooms
3 spring onions (scallions)
3 tablespoons vegetable oil
1½ tablespoons finely chopped
*   Sichuan pickles*
2½ tablespoons light soya sauce
1 tablespoon Hoisin sauce
1½ tablespoons Chinese mushroom
*   sauce*
½ tablespoon chilli sauce
3-4 tablespoons vegetable or
*   chicken stock*
1 teaspoon sugar
1 tablespoon rice wine or sherry

4-6 portions

THIS LIGHT, flavoursome dish can be used as a starter for a long multi-course meal.

Method: Cut each beancurd cake into 4-6 pieces. Poach in boiling water for 2 minutes. Lift them out with a slotted spoon, drain and place on a serving dish.

Cut each mushroom into quarters and spring onions into 1 cm (¼ in) diagonal sections. Heat oil in a wok or frying pan. When hot, add mushrooms, spring onions and pickles. Stir over medium heat for 1½ minutes. Add all the sauces, stock, sugar and rice wine or sherry and continue to stir-fry for 1½ minutes.

Serving: Pour the mushrooms and sauce over the beancurd on the serving plate. Toss them lightly together and serve.

BEANCURD WITH SESAME PASTE

Ma Jiang Doufu

4 cakes beancurd (tofu)
2½ tablespoons sesame paste or
  peanut butter
1 tablespoon sesame oil
1½ tablespoons vegetable oil
3 tablespoons light soya sauce
2 tablespoons rice wine vinegar
2 spring onions (scallions)

4-6 portions

I AM INCLUDING this comparatively simple dish as one of China's top dishes mainly because it is evocative of life and eating in China. When there is no great choice of dishes to present for a meal, this one should be included on the menu to appease hunger and warm the cockles of the heart!

Method: Cut each cake of beancurd into 6 cubes and spread out on a serving dish. Mix the sesame paste or peanut butter with the sesame oil and vegetable oil until well blended. Mix the soya sauce with the vinegar. Diagonally chop the spring onions into 1 cm (¼ in) sections.

Serving: Place a dollop of the sesame paste and oil mixture on top of each piece of beancurd, and pour a dash of soya sauce and vinegar mixture over them. The diner uses a chopstick to mash or rub the beancurd into the soya and vinegar sauce and the sesame paste, and eats them with boiled rice or congee.

SICHUAN MA PO BEANCURD

Si Chuan Ma Po Doufu

3-4 cakes beancurd (tofu)
2 tablespoons salted black beans
4 tablespoons vegetable oil
180 g (6 oz) minced or ground
*   pork or beef*
Salt to taste
Pepper to taste
3 slices root ginger, finely chopped
60 g (2 oz) Sichuan pickles,
*   chopped*
3 spring onions (scallions), chopped
2 dried red chillies
5 tablespoons chicken stock
2 tablespoons light soya sauce
1 tablespoon chilli sauce
1 tablespoon Sichuan hot bean
*   paste (optional)*
2 tablespoons rice wine or sherry
1 tablespoon cornflour (cornstarch)
*   blended with 3 tablespoons*
*   water*
2 teaspoons sesame oil

4-6 portions with other dishes

THIS IS A SIMPLE but distinctive dish of the common people. First cooked by a woman who had a pock-marked face — for that is what *ma po* means in Chinese — it has always been popular in the East and is now gaining recognition in the West.

Method: Cut the beancurd into dice. Soak black beans in warm water for 5 minutes, then drain and finely chop.

Heat oil in a wok or frying pan. When hot, add the meat, salt and pepper and stir-fry over high heat for 2 minutes. Add black beans, ginger, pickles, spring onions and chillies and mix together over high heat for another 2 minutes. Add stock, soya sauce, chilli sauce, hot bean paste and rice wine or sherry. Stir the mixture into sauce. Add the beancurd cubes to the sauce and turn them over to coat with sauce. Cook gently for 3 minutes. Add cornflour mixture and sesame oil. Stir the contents over medium heat for 1 minute and serve.

Serving: Serve in a deep serving bowl with ample rice.

RED-COOKED BEANCURD FROM THE FAMILY KITCHEN

Jia Chang Doufu

120-155 g (4-5 oz) Red-Cooked
    Pork (page 125)
3 cakes beancurd (tofu)
3-4 medium dried black
    mushrooms
2 medium zucchinis (courgettes)
3 tablespoons vegetable oil
1 medium onion, thinly sliced
2 slices root ginger, shredded
150 mL (¼ pt) chicken stock
3 tablespoons light soya sauce
1 tablespoon oyster sauce
1 tablespoon hoisin sauce
45 g (1½ oz) Sichuan pickles,
    finely chopped
2 teaspoons sugar
1 tablespoon cornflour (cornstarch)
    blended with 4 tablespoons
    water

4-5 portions

WE CHINESE ARE fond of using up all the bits and pieces of food leftover from previous meals. Hence there are often "recreated" dishes on the Chinese dining table. Such dishes are made up of a main ingredient cooked with several leftover ingredients. Here, for example, a small amount of Red-Cooked Pork is enhanced by dried mushrooms and pickles, which transform the neutral-tasting beancurd. This is a very flavoursome dish.

Method: Cut pork into bite-size pieces. Cut each piece of beancurd into 8 pieces. Soak dried mushrooms in hot water for 30 minutes. Drain, remove stems and cut caps into quarters. Cut zucchini diagonally into 1.5 cm (½ in) segments.

Heat oil in a wok or frying pan. When hot, add onion, ginger and mushrooms. Stir-fry them over medium heat for 1½ minutes. Add the pork, zucchinis and beancurd. Shallow-fry together for 2½ minutes, turning the contents over. Add the stock, soya sauce, oyster sauce, hoisin sauce, pickles and sugar. Bring contents to a gentle boil. Simmer for 5-6 minutes. Add the blended cornflour. Stir and turn the contents a few times and serve.

Serving: Serve in a large serving bowl and let diners help themselves.

DEEP-FRIED BEANCURD WITH BACON, MUSHROOMS AND EGGS

Yan Rou Doufu

3 cakes beancurd (tofu)
3 eggs
Salt to taste
250 g (8 oz) fresh mushrooms
1 medium capsicum (bell pepper)
Oil for deep-frying
2 tablespoons vegetable oil
2 slices bacon, cut into matchsticks
200 mL (⅓ pt) chicken stock
1 tablespoon cornflour (cornstarch)
   blended with ¾ tablespoon
   water
1 tablespoon light soya sauce
1½ tablespoons chopped spring
   onions (scallions)
2 teaspoons sesame oil

5-6 portions with other dishes

THIS INEXPENSIVE, flavoursome dish is ideal for a family meal.

Method: Cut each piece of beancurd into 6 pieces. Beat eggs lightly with salt. Remove mushroom stems, clean caps and cut each into quarters. Seed and cut capsicum into 1.5 cm (½ in) slices.

Heat oil to a depth of 1.5-2.5 cm (½-1 in) in a wok or frying pan and deep-fry the beancurd pieces for 2½-3 minutes. Remove with a slotted utensil and set aside. Heat vegetable oil in a wok. When hot, add bacon and mushrooms, and stir-fry for 2 minutes. Add capsicum and stir-fry for 1 more minute. Pour in the beaten eggs. Stir them gently with the other ingredients over medium heat. When the eggs are almost set, add the deep-fried beancurd pieces. Stir and turn them to scramble with the eggs. Pour in the stock, bring to a boil, and stir ingredients together. Simmer over medium heat, stirring several times. Pour the blended cornflour and soya sauce evenly over the contents, and stir them a couple of times.

Serving: Serve in a well-heated deep-sided bowl, and sprinkle with chopped spring onions and sesame oil at the table.

STIR-FRIED BEANCURD WITH SEAFOOD
Hai Xian Doufu

3 cakes beancurd (tofu)
1½ tablespoons dried prawns
(shrimps)
3 spring onions (scallions)
10 medium mussels
3½ tablespoons vegetable oil
3 slices root ginger, shredded
3 slices onion
120 g (4 oz) cooked crabmeat,
flaked
Salt to taste
Pepper to taste
4 tablespoons chicken stock
1½ tablespoons light soya sauce
1 tablespoon oyster sauce
2 tablespoons rice wine
1 tablespoon cornflour (cornstarch)
blended with 4 tablespoons
water

4-6 portions

THIS IS AN extraordinarily savoury dish.

Method: Cut beancurd into 2.5 cm (1 in) dice. Soak dried prawns in hot water for 10 minutes, then drain and chop coarsely. Chop spring onions coarsely, dividing the green parts from the white. Clean and poach the mussels in boiling water for 3 minutes. Drain and remove from their shells.

Heat oil in a wok or frying pan. When hot, add ginger, onion, the white parts of the spring onions and the dried prawns. Stir-fry them over medium heat for 1 minute. Add the crabmeat, mussels and beancurd. Season with salt and pepper, and stir gently for 1½ minutes. Add the stock, soya sauce, oyster sauce and rice wine. Continue to stir over medium heat for 2 minutes. Sprinkle the contents with the blended cornflour and the green of the chopped spring onions; stir and turn once more.

Serving: This dish should be eaten hot. Serve on a well-heated plate and accompany with rice.

STIRRED EGGS
Liu Wang Cai

3 eggs
300 mL (1⅓ cups) strong chicken
   stock
1½ tablespoons cornflour
   (cornstarch) blended with 4
   tablespoons water
Salt to taste
2½ tablespoons vegetable oil
2 teaspoons sesame oil
3 tablespoons green peas

4-5 portions

THIS TYPICAL BEIJING (Peking) dish is very
comforting during a Beijing winter. Although there
are many dishes in China which complement rice,
this is the only one which is actually poured on to the
rice when eaten.

Method: Break the eggs into a large bowl and beat for
10 seconds. Add the stock, blended cornflour, salt and
2 teaspoons of vegetable oil. Continue to beat for 10
seconds until the mixture is well mixed.
   Heat remaining oil in a saucepan over low heat.
When it is hot, slowly pour in the beaten egg mixture
in a thin stream, stirring all the time. Add the
sesame oil and peas and continue to stir and cook
slowly until the eggs are just set.

Serving: Pour the contents of the saucepan into a
large serving bowl and bring it to the dining table for
the diners to help themselves.

STIR-FRIED OMELETTE WITH TOMATOES
Xian Qie Chao Dan

5 eggs
Salt to taste
Pepper to taste
5 medium tomatoes
5 tablespoons vegetable oil
1½ tablespoons light soya sauce
2 spring onions (scallions), coarsely
  chopped

4-5 portions with other dishes

JUST AS THERE is a profusion of Chinese (celery) cabbage in Beijing (Peking) in winter, so there is a profusion of tomatoes in the summer. There is little wonder then that tomatoes are frequently used in Chinese cooking. In this simple but prized dish, the tomatoes are teamed with another food commonly available in the Chinese kitchen: eggs.

Method: Break eggs into a bowl. Add salt and pepper to taste. Beat until well mixed. Immerse the tomatoes in boiling water, then drain, peel and cut into quarters.

Heat oil in a wok or frying pan over medium heat. Tilt the pan so the oil evenly covers the surface. When hot, add the eggs and cook until almost set; push them to one side of the pan and add the tomatoes to the opposite side. When the eggs are completely set, turn and scramble lightly with the tomatoes.

Serving: Sprinkle the contents of the pan with soya sauce and chopped spring onions and serve.

WANG PU MULTI-LAYERED OMELETTE
Wang Pu Chao Dan

8 eggs
Salt to taste
Pepper to taste
2 tablespoons chopped spring
    onions (scallions)
125 mL (½ cup) vegetable oil
1½ tablespoons rice wine or sherry
1½ tablespoons light soya sauce

5-6 portions

THIS DISH ORIGINATED with the boat-dwellers of Wang Pu, a city on the Pearl River. Although basic, it has become so well liked that it is now on the menu of many famous restaurants in the region. Its fascination lies in its interspersed layers of soft and well-cooked eggs flavoured by freshly chopped spring onions and wine.

Method: Break eggs into a bowl. Add salt and pepper to taste and half the chopped spring onions. Beat until well mixed.

Heat a third of the oil in a wok or small frying pan. Tilt the pan so the oil evenly covers its surface. Pour in a third of the beaten egg. Before it sets, sprinkle over remaining spring onions. When the eggs are about to set completely, transfer the omelette with the aid of a spatula to a well-heated serving plate.

Repeat the process by adding and heating the second third of the oil into the now empty pan, followed by pouring in the second third of the beaten egg. When the second omelette has cooked but is still very soft on top, use a spatula to place it on the serving plate on top of the first omelette. Repeat with the third omelette. When all three omelettes are cooked and in place, sprinkle the top with the combined heated wine and soya sauce, and the balance of the spring onions.

Serving: To be fully appreciated and enjoyed, this dish should be served and eaten with plain boiled rice.

STIR-FRIED EGGS WITH PEPPERED PRAWNS

Ha Yen Chao Dan

5 eggs
Salt to taste
Pepper to taste
*2 spring onions (scallions), finely
    chopped*
*250-375 g (½-¾ lb) prawns
    (shrimps), shelled and deveined*
½ teaspoon freshly ground pepper
1 egg white, lightly beaten
1 tablespoon cornflour (cornstarch)
6 tablespoons vegetable oil
1 tablespoon rice wine or sherry

4-5 portions

THOUGH NOT ONE of the most refined dishes, Stir-fried Eggs with Peppered Prawns (Shrimps) is extremely appetizing.

Method: Beat eggs lightly. Add salt, pepper and spring onions. Beat again to combine ingredients. Sprinkle prawns with freshly ground pepper. Dip in egg white and dust with cornflour.

Heat 4 tablespoons oil in a wok or frying pan. When hot, add prawns and stir over medium heat for 1½ minutes; push them to one side away from the centre of the heat. Add the remaining 2 tablespoons oil and tilt pan so the oil evenly covers its surface. Pour in the beaten egg. As soon as it begins to set, stir in the prawns and scramble for 1½ minutes over medium heat.

Serving: Sprinkle the contents of the pan with rice wine or sherry and serve with boiled rice. The alcohol striking the prawns and egg at high heat will release an appetizing aroma.

YELLOW FLOWER PORK

Mu Shu Rou

4 eggs
Salt to taste
Pepper to taste
3 tablespoons dry wood ear fungus
4-5 medium dried black
   mushrooms
2 spring onions (scallions)
90 g (3 oz) snow peas (mange tout)
120 g (4 oz) canned bamboo shoots
120 g (4 oz) pork belly (fresh bacon
   or side pork)
5 tablespoons vegetable oil
3 tablespoons chicken stock
2 tablespoons dark soya sauce
1 tablespoon rice wine or sherry
1 teaspoon sesame oil

4-5 portions

ALMOST ANY CHINESE stir-fried dish can be combined with eggs to form a new recipe. The best known of these is probably the savoury and aromatic Yellow Flower Pork. It is often served and eaten wrapped in pancakes.

Method: Break eggs into a bowl. Add salt and pepper. Beat well with a fork or a pair of chopsticks. Rinse wood ears, soak in hot water for 5 minutes, then drain. Soak dried black mushrooms in hot water for 30 minutes. Drain and cut mushroom caps into quarters. Diagonally cut spring onions, snow peas and bamboo shoots into 4 cm (1½ in) sections. Cut pork into thin slices 5 x 2.5 cm (2 x 1 in).

   Heat 4 tablespoons of oil in a wok or frying pan. When hot, add the pork and stir-fry over high heat for 2 minutes. Add mushrooms, wood ears, snow peas, bamboo shoots and spring onions. Stir-fry for 3 minutes. Pour the stock and soya sauce over the contents of the pan and stir-fry together for 1½ minutes. Remove the pan from the heat.

   Heat remaining 1 tablespoon oil in a separate wok or frying pan over medium heat. When hot, pour in the beaten eggs. Stir a few times, allowing the eggs time to set slowly. When the eggs are set break them up into 2.5-4 cm (1-1½ in) size pieces, and turn them into the pan containing the vegetables. Stir them over medium heat with the pork, vegetables and gravy to allow the eggs to absorb some of the flavours of the pork and the gravy. Adjust the flavouring by adding rice wine or sherry and sesame oil. Stir-fry gently for 30 seconds and serve.

SALT EGGS, SOYA EGGS, TEA EGGS, 100-YEAR-OLD EGGS

Xian Dan, Lu Shui Dan, Cha Ye Dan, Pi Dan

TO THE CHINESE palate, eggs are an ideal complement to rice. These four types of eggs are eaten with congee — the salty and pickled flavours of the eggs complement the sweet and refreshing character of soft rice.

Salt Eggs: Generally larger than chicken eggs and pale blue in colour, these are usually hard-boiled duck eggs which have been soaked in brine for varying lengths of time. When cracked open, the yolk is bright orange. They are usually served cut through the shells into six segments.

Soya Eggs are hard-boiled eggs that have been cooked in soya sauce, or in the rich gravy of a red-cooked meat dish, such as pork knuckles (hocks), pork trotters (pigs' feet) and beef shin (shank). After cooking for 30 minutes, the egg will assume a rich dark brown skin, which contrasts perfectly with congee both in taste and colour.

Tea Eggs or *Marble Eggs* are hard-boiled eggs with cracked shells that are soaked, boiled or simmered in strong tea. The tea seeps through the cracks in the shell and produces a marbled pattern on the white of the hard-boiled egg.

100-Year-Old Eggs, also called *1000-Year-Old Eggs,* or *Song Hua Dan* or *Pine Flower Eggs,* seem to intrigue Western taste-buds and imaginations. The egg whites are dark green in colour with bright yellowish-green yolks. They taste cheesy and are unmistakably smelly! Usually bought in food shops, they are very seldom made at home.

However, here is the recipe. To make a dozen *100-year-old eggs*, dissolve 4 tablespoons sea salt in 450 mL (2 cups) of water, gradually add 250 mL (1 cup) pine ash and 5 tablespoons lime. Stir them into a smooth mixture. Wash 12 duck eggs in warm water. Coat them completely with a 6-cm (2½-in) mud pack. Be sure that each egg is completely covered. Roll the mud-covered eggs in a tray of husks or chopped straw so that they are coated, thus preventing them from sticking to each other. Carefully arrange the eggs in a pile at the bottom of a large earthenware jar. Cover them with a lid.

After 3 days, take the eggs out and rearrange them, moving those on the top to the bottom of the pile, and vice versa. Repeat the procedure 5 times in 15 days. After that period of changing and re-arranging, seal the jar by placing the lid on firmly and leaving the eggs to stand undisturbed for 1 month. After this time, the eggs should be ready for use. The mixture of salt, lime and ash slowly cooks the eggs and acts as a time-machine to shorten the cooking time from 100 years to 50 days! The eggs, now covered in husks, straw and grey mud, will appear remarkably like antique eggs.

Serving: To serve and eat the eggs, wash off the husks, mud and straw under running water and crack the shells gently. Remove the shells and cut the eggs lengthwise into quarters. Served with these eggs, congee will taste twice as pure and refreshing to the early-morning palate.

BASIC STEAMED EGGS

Zheng Shui Dan

3 eggs
450 mL (2 cups) strong chicken
   stock
Salt to taste
1½ tablespoons chopped spring
   onions (scallions)
1½ tablespoons light soya sauce

4-6 portions

A POPULAR WAY of preparing eggs in China is to make a savoury custard which blends well with plain boiled rice. When beaten eggs are mixed with water or stock and steamed into a custard, this produces a dish even lighter than scrambled eggs, as no oil is used. Many Chinese have fond memories of this dish, as it is often served to the very young, the very old and to invalids.

Method: Beat the eggs with a fork or a pair of chopsticks for 15 seconds. Combine them with the stock and salt. Stir until the mixture is well blended. Pour into a heatproof bowl.

Place the bowl in a steamer and steam over boiling water for 25 minutes. Alternatively, place the bowl in 5 cm (2 in) of hot water in a saucepan, cover and bring the water in the saucepan to a gentle boil. Allow the contents of the bowl to steam for 20 minutes, when the savoury egg custard should be ready to serve.

Serving: Bring the bowl to the dining table. The top of the custard should be firm. Sprinkle the top with the chopped spring onions and soya sauce.

FOUR VARIETIES OF STEAMED EGGS
Si Wei Zheng Dan

2 eggs
Salt to taste
450 mL (2 cups) chicken stock
1 teaspoon vegetable oil
2 salt eggs
2 soya eggs
Two 100-year-old eggs
1 dried sausage (lop chang) or
*   1 slice bacon*
1¼ tablespoons chopped spring
*   onions (scallions)*
1¼ tablespoons light soya sauce

4-5 portions

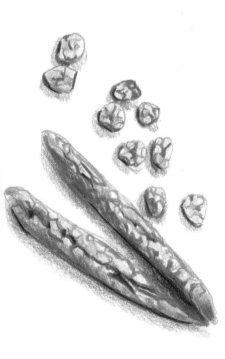

STEAMED SAVOURY EGG custards can be made into fancier versions simply by blending seafood, flaked fish or minced meat into the beaten eggs and stock before the mixture is steamed in a basin. Such dishes are part of the daily diet of many Chinese.

One of the most interesting steamed egg custards is Four Varieties of Steamed Eggs. In this recipe, salt eggs, soya eggs and 100-year-old eggs are diced and combined with beaten eggs and dried sausage.

Method: Prepare the egg custard mixture in the same manner as Basic Steamed Eggs (page 80). Cut or dice the salt eggs, soya eggs and 100-year-old eggs into small cubes or segments. Cut the sausage or bacon into thin slices. Line the bottom of a heatproof casserole with the diced egg cubes interspersed with slices of sausage. Pour the beaten egg custard mixture over them. Place the casserole in a steamer, or partly immerse in boiling water in a large covered saucepan, and steam steadily for 20-25 minutes.

Serving: Bring the casserole directly from the steamer or pan to the table. Sprinkle the top of the custard with spring onions and soya sauce.
The diners should help themselves by digging into the savoury custard and adding spoonfuls to their own bowl of rice.

FU RONG CAULIFLOWER

Fu Rong Cai Hua

1 tablespoon dried prawns
   (shrimps)
600 mL (2⅔ cups) chicken stock
Salt to taste
1 medium cauliflower, in florets

SAUCE

2 egg whites
150 mL (⅔ cup) chicken stock
2 tablespoons minced raw chicken
   breast
Pepper to taste
2 tablespoons vegetable oil
1½ tablespoons cornflour
   (cornstarch) blended with
   5 tablespoons milk

2 tablespoons finely chopped ham

4-5 portions

FOR SOME UNSPECIFIED reason, in the West all
Chinese dishes which include eggs are called fu
yungs. In China, the term is Fu Rong and it refers
to dishes in which beaten egg white is blended with
stock to make a sauce. Sometimes minced chicken
breast or minced white fish is added to the beaten
egg white to make the fu rong dishes richer. In the
West, a small amount of cream may be added to
enhance the richness of the sauce.

Method: Soak dried prawns in hot water for
15 minutes and drain.

Heat stock in a saucepan. Add salt, dried prawns
and cauliflower florets. Bring to the boil, lower heat
and simmer gently for 8 minutes. Drain.

To make the sauce, beat egg whites for 10 seconds.
Add the stock, minced chicken and pepper, and beat
together for 5-6 seconds. Heat oil in another
saucepan. When hot, slowly stir in the egg white
mixture in a thin stream. When the mixture comes to
the boil, add the cornflour and milk to thicken the
sauce. Continue to stir over low heat for 2 minutes.

Serving: Place the cauliflower mixture in a deep bowl.
Pour the sauce over it and sprinkle with chopped
ham.

FU RONG CHINESE CABBAGE

Fu Rong Bai Cai

2 tablespoons dried prawns
   (shrimps)
600 mL (2⅔ cups) chicken stock
Salt to taste
1 medium Chinese (celery)
   cabbage, chopped

SAUCE

2 egg whites
150 mL (⅔ cup) chicken stock
2 tablespoons minced raw chicken
   breast
Pepper to taste
2 tablespoons vegetable oil
1½ tablespoons cornflour
   (cornstarch) blended with
   5 tablespoons milk

2 tablespoons finely chopped ham

4-5 portions

THE FULL SPLENDOUR of the Chinese cabbage, which is grown in profusion in North China in the winter especially around the Beijing (Peking) area, can only be appreciated when it is eaten in quantity. It is the one food which can be fully enjoyed without meat, fish or seafood when consumed with rice.

Method: The cabbage can be cooked in precisely the same manner as cauliflower in the previous recipe, except that it will need to be simmered for another 5 minutes with an extra tablespoon of dried prawns, soaked, and in serving, none of the cooking liquid needs to be drained away. Otherwise, simply follow exactly the same procedure.

   Although only a small amount of meat is used in this recipe, it seems like a very meaty dish, and it is most enjoyable eaten with a large amount of plain rice.

FISH AND SEAFOOD

FISH AND SEAFOOD

CHINA HAS several mighty rivers with thousands of tributaries and a winding coastline more than 4800 kilometres (3000 miles) long, so it is not surprising to discover that fish and seafood are consumed often. We also have been fish farming since time immemorial. Every village in China seems to have a pond or small lake. These are drained once a year and the fully grown fish are taken out to be used or sold for food. The smaller fish are returned to the reflooded ponds to grow for another season.

When cooking fish, we Chinese seldom stir-fry it, as it breaks up too easily. Fish is more often steamed, as steam is readily available in a Chinese kitchen, and most fish can be cooked successfully by this method. Fish is also cooked by shallow-frying or pan-frying, followed by braising. Seafood also is often cooked by quick stir-frying.

We Chinese do not feel that the flavours of meat, fish and seafood need to be exclusive of each other. They are often used in conjunction with each other; indeed it is when the two flavours are blended that the most savoury dishes are created.

To reduce the fishy flavour in fish and seafood dishes, we often use ginger and other strong-tasting vegetables and herbs. Fish-based sauces such as shrimp sauce and oyster sauce, are seldom used in fish and seafood cookery; this is mainly to avoid doubling up on the fishy flavours. Indeed, in concocting seafood sauces or making fish soups, chicken stock is normally used.

RED-COOKED FISH STEAKS

Hong Shao Yu

700-900 g (1½-2 lb) fish such as cod, halibut, turbot, bream or seabass, cut into large chunks
Salt to taste
Pepper to taste
1 egg white, lightly beaten
1½ tablespoons cornflour (cornstarch)
5 slices root ginger, shredded

SAUCE

4 tablespoons dark soya sauce
2 teaspoons sugar
2 tablespoons stock
2 tablespoons rice wine or sherry

5 tablespoons vegetable oil
5 spring onions (scallions), cut into fine shreds

4-6 portions with other dishes

THESE FISH STEAKS with ginger and onion sauce make a simple but tasty meal.

Method: Sprinkle the fish with salt and pepper, dip in egg white and dust with cornflour. Mix half of the shredded ginger with the soya sauce, sugar, stock and rice wine or sherry until they are well blended; set aside.

Heat oil in a frying pan with a lid. When hot, sprinkle the oil evenly with remaining shredded ginger, and place the fish in the pan. Shallow-fry over medium heat for 2 minutes, then turn the fish over with a spatula to fry on the opposite side for 2 minutes. Drain away any excess oil, and pour in the sauce. Top with half the spring onions. Cover and cook gently for 3 minutes.

Serving: Transfer the fish to a serving plate and pour sauce from the pan on top of each piece of fish and sprinkle them with some spring onion shreds.

STEAMED WHOLE FISH

Zhang Yu

*1 whole seabass or bream, or any
    firm-fleshed fish weighing about
    2.25 kg (4½ lb)*
1 tablespoon vegetable oil
Salt to taste
Pepper to taste
6 spring onions (scallions)
6 slices root ginger
2 tablespoons light soya sauce
2 tablespoons rice wine or sherry
3 tablespoons vegetable oil

7-8 portions with other dishes

THIS RECIPE BRINGS out the full flavour of fish.

Method: Clean the fish thoroughly. Rub it inside and
out with oil and sprinkle with salt and pepper.
Cut the spring onions and ginger into double
matchsticks. Place the fish lengthwise on a heatproof
oval dish, and over the top of the fish sprinkle a thick
layer of half the spring onion and ginger matchsticks
mixed together.

Place the dish into a preheated steamer and steam
on high heat for 25 minutes. Remove the dish from
the steamer. Brush away the already steamed ginger
and spring onions from the top of the fish and replace
with the remaining spring onions and ginger.
Pour away half the liquid from the bottom of
the dish.

Serving: Sprinkle the entire fish with light soya
sauce and rice wine or sherry. Heat the oil until it is
very hot (near boiling) and pour it in a small stream
over the length of the fish through the layer of ginger
shreds and spring onions. Serve at once.

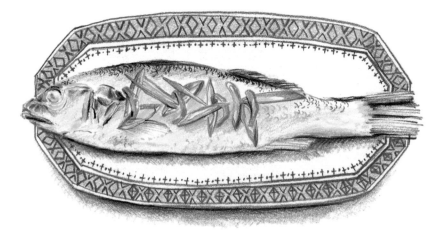

SICHUAN BEAN PASTE FISH
Si Chuan Dou Ban Yu

*2 medium red and green
    capsicums (bell peppers)*
2 tablespoons salted black beans
3 cloves garlic, coarsely chopped
3 slices root ginger, shredded

*1.25-1.5 kg (2½-3 lb) whole fish
    such as seabass, bream, carp or
    trout*
Salt to taste
Pepper to taste
Oil for deep-frying

2 tablespoons vegetable oil
2 medium onions, thinly sliced
*2 fresh chillies, seeded and finely
    chopped*
120 g (4 oz) minced or ground pork
2 tablespoons light soya sauce
4 tablespoons chicken stock
2 teaspoons sugar
2 tablespoons rice wine or sherry
*2½ teaspoons Sichuan hot bean
    paste*
150 mL (⅔ cup) boiling water

5-6 portions with other dishes

THIS FISH DISH has a distinctive Sichuan flavour.

Method: Remove the seeds from the capsicums and
cut into 5 x 1 cm (2 x ¼ in) strips. Soak black beans
in 4 tablespoons hot water for 15 minutes, then mash
them with the chopped garlic and ginger.

Score the fish on either side with half a dozen deep
cuts. Sprinkle with salt and pepper. Heat oil to a
depth of 5 cm (2 in) in a deep-fryer and fry the fish
for 5-6 minutes, or until slightly crisp, then drain
and set aside.

To make the sauce, heat the oil in a wok or frying
pan. When hot, add the onions and stir-fry for
1 minute. Add the mashed black beans, garlic and
ginger, together with the chillies. Stir and mix over
high heat for 1½ minutes. Stir in pork. Pour in the
soya sauce, stock, sugar, rice wine or sherry and the
hot bean paste. Cook for 3-4 minutes, stirring now
and then. Pour in boiling water to dilute the contents.
Bring to boiling point.

Place the fish in the bubbling sauce. Baste the fish
with the sauce. Add the strips of capsicum on either
side of the fish. Cover and allow the contents to cook
gently for 5-6 minutes.

Serving: Transfer the fish to a well-heated serving
plate. Spoon the minced pork and other ingredients,
including the capsicums, on top of the fish as
garnish.

TRIPLE FRY OF THREE DELICIOUSNESS WITH BLACK BEANS

Dou Chi Chao San Xian

*150 g (¹/₃ lb) king prawns (large
    shrimps), shelled and deveined*
5-6 sea scallops
*90-100 g (3-4 oz) squid or boneless
    chicken*
4 teaspoons salted black beans
2 spring onions (scallions)
½ red capsicum (bell pepper)
6 tablespoons vegetable oil
3 slices root ginger, shredded
2 cloves garlic, crushed
½ teaspoon chilli sauce
1 tablespoon light soya sauce
5 tablespoons chicken stock
*¾ tablespoon cornflour (cornstarch)
    blended with 3 tablespoons
    water*
1 teaspoon sesame oil
1 tablespoon rice wine or sherry

4-5 portions with other dishes

THE THREE MAIN ingredients — prawns, scallops and
squid — give this dish its poetic name.

Method: Cut each prawn into 2-3 sections, scallops
into halves, and squid or chicken into similar-size
pieces. Soak black beans in hot water for 10 minutes.
Drain and chop coarsely. Cut the spring onions
diagonally into 2.5 cm (1 in) sections and the
capsicum into 2.5 x 1.5 cm (1 x ½ in) pieces.

Heat 4 tablespoons oil in a wok or frying pan.
When very hot, add the prawns, scallops and squid or
chicken. Stir-fry over high heat for 1½ minutes.
Remove with a slotted spoon and set aside. Pour 2
tablespoons remaining oil into the wok. Add the
ginger, garlic and black beans. Stir over high heat for
30 seconds. Add chilli sauce, soya sauce and stock.
Return the prawns, scallops and squid to the pan.
Stir into the sauce over high heat for 30 seconds.
Sprinkle the contents with blended cornflour, sesame
oil and wine. Stir for 30 seconds.

Serving: This dish should be served hot on a heated
plate.

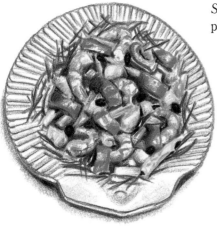

STIR-FRIED KING PRAWNS

Chao Ha Qiu

375 g (¾ lb) king prawns (large
   shrimps), shelled and deveined
Salt to taste
½ egg white, lightly beaten
1 tablespoon cornflour (cornstarch)
6 tablespoons vegetable oil
3 slices root ginger, shredded
2 cloves garlic, crushed
½ medium onion, very thinly
   sliced
6 tablespoons chicken stock
1 tablespoon light soya sauce
4-5 tablespoons green peas
1 tablespoon rice wine or sherry
1 teaspoon sesame oil
Pepper to taste
1 tablespoon cornflour (cornstarch)
   blended with 3 tablespoons
   water

4-5 portions with other dishes

THIS SAVOURY DISH can be eaten with a wide variety of other dishes, irrespective of their basic flavours. Easy and quick to cook, it ranks as one of the most popular party dishes in China.

Method: Wash the prawns. Sprinkle with salt, dip in egg white and dust with cornflour.

Heat 4 tablespoons oil in a wok or frying pan over high heat. When hot, add ginger, garlic and onion and stir-fry for 15 seconds. Add prawns and stir-fry for 1¼ minutes. Remove the prawns with a slotted spoon and set aside. Add stock, soya sauce and peas to the pan. When contents reboil, cook for 3 minutes, stirring several times. Return the prawns to the clear bubbling sauce. Sprinkle with rice wine or sherry, sesame oil, pepper to taste and blended cornflour. Stir over high heat for 15 seconds and serve.

CHILLI PRAWNS

La Jiao Ha

*500 g (1 lb) king prawns (large
    shrimps), shelled and deveined*
Salt to taste
Pepper to taste
1 egg white, lightly beaten
*1½ tablespoons cornflour
    (cornstarch)*
1 tablespoon rice wine or sherry
150 mL (⅔ cup) oil for frying
*1 small fresh green chilli, seeded
    and chopped*
*2 small dried red chillies, seeded
    and chopped*
3 slices root ginger, chopped
*2 spring onions (scallions),
    diagonally chopped*
1 tablespoon yellow bean paste
1 tablespoon light soya sauce
1 teaspoon sugar
1½ tablespoons chicken stock
*1 tablespoon cornflour (cornstarch)
    blended with 3 tablespoons
    water*
1 teaspoon sesame oil

4-6 portions with other dishes

THIS IS A SPICY dish, full of zest. Serve as a contrast to the more neutral-tasting dishes which often form the main part of a multi-course Chinese dinner.

Method: Rinse prawns under running water and drain well. Place the prawns in a bowl with salt, pepper, egg white, cornflour and rice wine or sherry, and mix them well.

Heat oil in a wok or deep frying pan. When hot, add the prawns and stir-fry over medium heat for 2 minutes. Remove with a slotted spoon, set aside and drain. Pour away most of the oil, leaving 2 tablespoons at the bottom of the pan.

Heat this remaining oil over medium heat. When hot, add the chillies, ginger and spring onions, and stir-fry for 30 seconds. Add the yellow bean paste, soya sauce, sugar and stock. Stir and mix them together over high heat for 15 seconds. Return the prawns to the bubbling sauce and stir. Sprinkle the contents with blended cornflour and sesame oil. Stir once more and serve.

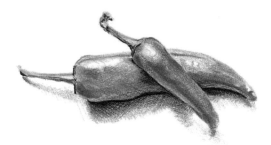

SICHUAN CHILLI SQUID

Si Chuan La Jiao You Yu

500 g (1 lb) fresh squid
Salt to taste
Pepper to taste
1 small red capsicum (bell pepper)
1 small green capsicum (bell pepper)
3 tablespoons vegetable oil
3 slices root ginger, coarsely chopped
3 cloves garlic, coarsely chopped

SAUCE

2 tablespoons vegetable oil
2 tablespoons yellow bean paste
2 tablespoons Sichuan hot bean paste
1½ tablespoons light soya sauce
1 tablespoon tomato purée
1½ tablespoons rice wine or sherry
1 tablespoon cornflour (cornstarch) blended with 3 tablespoons water

4-6 portions with other dishes

IN THIS DISH the spicy sauce adds flavour and the squid texture. The speed with which you cook the squid determines the texture — the faster it is cooked, the more tender it will be.

Method: Clean the squid: Cut out the central head section and discard along with the innards, the round cartilage and the cuttlebone. Rinse under running water. Drain and cut into 4 x 2 cm (1½ x ¾ in) strips. Score with criss-cross cuts (cutting halfway through each strip of squid 6 times). Sprinkle with salt and pepper. Cut the capsicums into the same size pieces as the squid.

Heat oil in a wok or frying pan. When hot, add the ginger and garlic and stir. Add the squid and stir over high heat for 1 minute; remove and set aside.

To make the sauce, add oil to the wok. When hot, add yellow bean paste, Sichuan hot bean paste, soya sauce, tomato purée, wine or sherry and blended cornflour. Stir until the sauce thickens. Add the capsicums and return the squid to the wok. Stir over high heat for 1 minute and serve.

STIR-FRIED EGGS WITH SCALLOPS

Fu Zhou Dai Zi

3 spring onions (scallions)
4 tablespoons vegetable oil
250 g (½ lb) fresh sea scallops,
  shelled
Salt to taste
Pepper to taste
1½ tablespoons rice wine or sherry
3 eggs, beaten
2 tablespoons finely chopped ham

4-6 portions

AS WITH ALL CHINESE COOKED seafood meals, this dish should be consumed hot. The last-moment addition of chopped spring onions enhances the aromatic appeal of the dish.

Method: Chop the spring onions finely, dividing the white parts from the green.

Heat 3 tablespoons of oil in a wok or frying pan. When hot, add the scallops and the white of the spring onions. Stir-fry over medium heat for nearly 1 minute. Add salt, pepper and rice wine or sherry. Continue to stir-fry for 1 minute. Remove the mixture from the wok and set aside.

Add remaining 1 tablespoon oil to the wok. When hot, pour in the beaten eggs. Stir them a few times, but before they have set, return the scallops to the wok. Sprinkle the contents with the spring onion greens and chopped ham. Stir them together for 15 seconds, then serve.

CRAB IN HOT BLACK BEAN SAUCE

Chi Jiao Xie

1.25 kg (2½ lbs) fresh crabs
2 tablespoons salted black beans
3 cloves garlic, finely chopped
5-6 spring onions (scallions)
5-6 slices root ginger, shredded
2 fresh red chillies, seeded and
  chopped
Salt to taste
1½ tablespoons rice wine or sherry
5-6 tablespoons vegetable oil
3 tablespoons chicken stock
2 tablespoons rice wine vinegar
½ tablespoon sugar
1½ tablespoons light soya sauce
2 eggs, beaten
1 tablespoon cornflour (cornstarch)
  blended with 3 tablespoons
  water
1½ teaspoons sesame oil

4-5 portions with other dishes

JUSTICE CAN ONLY be done to this dish by eating it with your fingers.

Method: Scrub and clean crabs under running water. Break or chop each crab into 6-8 pieces, removing the gills. Crack the claws and legs with the back and side of the cleaver. Cut spring onions into 1 cm (½ in) sections. Soak the black beans in hot water for 10 minutes, and then drain, chop and crush. Place the crab pieces in a large bowl with half the garlic, spring onions, ginger, and chillies, and the salt, rice wine or sherry and black beans. Mix together and marinate for 30 minutes.

Heat oil in a wok or frying pan over high heat. When very hot, add the crab pieces and stir-fry over high heat for 3½ minutes. Remove and drain. Pour away any excess oil, leaving about 1½ tablespoons in the wok. Reheat; when hot, add the black beans and the remaining spring onions, ginger, garlic and chillies; stir over medium heat for 45 seconds. Add the stock, vinegar, sugar and soya sauce. When contents boil, return the crab pieces to the wok and stir over high heat for 2 minutes. Add the beaten eggs, pouring evenly over the contents. When the eggs set, sprinkle the contents with the blended cornflour and sesame oil. Stir until the sauce thickens. Serve.

CANTONESE ONION AND GINGER LOBSTER
Jiang Cong Long Ha

*1 lobster weighing about 700 g
(1½ lb)*
2 spring onions (scallions)
2 slices root ginger, finely chopped
1½ tablespoons rice wine or sherry

DIPPING SAUCE

2 spring onions (scallions)
2 slices root ginger, finely chopped
2 fresh chillies, seeded
2½ tablespoons vegetable oil
3 tablespoons light soya sauce
2 tablespoons rice wine vinegar
1 teaspoon sesame oil

3-4 portions with other dishes

THIS IS AN IDEAL recipe for those who like simply cooked fresh lobster.

Method: Wash and clean the lobster under running water. Cut lengthwise into halves, discarding the stomach and intestinal vein. Further cut lobster into 5 cm (2 in) sections. Finely chop the spring onions. Mix spring onions and ginger with the rice wine or sherry. Sprinkle the mixture on top of the lobster pieces. Place lobster pieces in a heatproof bowl.

Place the heatproof bowl in a steamer and steam vigorously for 10 minutes.

To prepare the dipping sauce, finely chop the spring onions and chillies. Arrange the spring onions, ginger and chillies in a heatproof bowl. Heat the oil in a small pan until smoking hot. Pour it over the contents of bowl and stir together. Pour in the soya sauce, vinegar and sesame oil. Mix well and serve.

Serving: The dipping sauce should be served on the table with the steamed lobster.

PEKING SLICED FISH IN WINE SAUCE

Jiu Liu Yu Pian

250 g (½ lb) fillet of sole, halibut or
    flounder
Salt to taste
1 egg white, lightly beaten
1½ tablespoons cornflour
    (cornstarch)
60 g (2 oz) wood ear fungus
Oil for deep-frying
2 slices root ginger

SAUCE

5 tablespoons chicken stock
1½ teaspoons sugar
3 tablespoons white wine
1 teaspoon vodka
½ tablespoon cornflour (cornstarch)
    blended with 2½ tablespoons
    water

4-5 portions with other dishes

THE WHITENESS of the fish contrasts with the jet
black wood ears in the translucent sauce — a refined
dish much seen on dining tables in Beijing (Peking).

Method: Cut fish into 4 x 2.5 cm (1½ x 1 in) slices.
Sprinkle with salt, dip in egg white and dust with
cornflour. Soak wood ears in hot water for 10 minutes
and drain.
   Heat oil to a depth of 1.5 cm (½ in) in a wok or deep
frying pan. When hot, reduce the heat to low, lay the
slices of fish evenly in the oil and cook for 1 minute
on each side. Remove the fish with a slotted spoon,
drain and set aside. Pour away the oil, leaving
2 tablespoons in the pan. Return pan to heat. Add
ginger and stir-fry for 30 seconds. Remove the ginger
with a slotted spoon. Add wood ears and stir-fry for
30 seconds.
   To make the sauce, combine all ingredients and
pour into the pan. Stir over medium heat until the
sauce thickens. Return the fish slices to the pan and
cook in the sauce, for 1½ minutes.

Serving: To serve, transfer the contents on to a well-
heated serving plate.

SQUIRREL FISH

Song Shu Yu

1 whole fish weighing about
   700-900 g (1½-2 lb)
Salt to taste
Pepper to taste
4 slices root ginger, finely chopped
3 tablespoons cornflour (cornstarch)
5 medium dried black mushrooms
3 tablespoons wood ear fungus
3 spring onions (scallions)
Oil for deep-frying
2 tablespoons vegetable oil
60 g (2 oz) canned bamboo shoots,
   chopped
1 slice bacon, finely chopped
3 tablespoons soya sauce
3 tablespoons chicken stock
2 tablespoons rice wine vinegar
1½ teaspoons sugar
2 tablespoons rice wine or sherry
1 tablespoon cornflour (cornstarch)
   blended with 4 tablespoons
   water

8-10 portions with other dishes

THIS FANCIFULLY NAMED dish is frequently served at dinner parties.

Method: Clean the fish and dry well. Slit open from head to tail on the underside. Cut 7-8 deep slashes on one side of the fish, and two similar slashes on the other side. Sprinkle fish inside and out with salt, pepper and ginger; coat with cornflour. Soak mushrooms and wood ear fungus separately in hot water for 30 minutes. Drain the wood ears and chop finely. Remove the tough stems from the mushrooms and cut caps into thin slices. Cut spring onions diagonally into 5 cm (2 in) sections.

Heat oil for deep-frying to a depth of 7½ cm (3 in) in a wok or deep-fryer. When hot, gently lower the fish, with the side cut twice facing up, and deep-fry for 3½-4 minutes. Reduce heat to low.

To make the sauce, heat vegetable oil in a wok or frying pan. When hot, add wood ears, dried mushrooms, bamboo shoots, bacon and spring onions. Stir-fry them over medium heat for 1¼ minutes. Add soya sauce, stock, vinegar, sugar, rice wine or sherry and cornflour. Stir-fry for 1 minute.

While the sauce is cooking, raise the heat of the oil in which the fish is being cooked in order to crisp the fish. In the process the tail of the fish will curl up due to the uneven number of cuts on either side of the fish. When this happens, lift the fish out of the hot oil, drain, and place on a well-heated serving plate. Raise the heat under the pan in which the sauce is being cooked. When the sauce bubbles, pour it over the crispy fish. At this point the fish will still be so hot that it will sizzle when the sauce is being poured over it. Serve immediately.

SWEET AND SOUR FISH

Tian Suan Yu

250 g (½ lb) fillet of fish
Salt to taste
½ medium red capsicum (bell
   pepper)
½ medium green capsicum (bell
   pepper)
1 slice pineapple

BATTER

1 egg
3 tablespoons all-purpose flour
2 tablespoons self-rising flour
Salt to taste
Milk

SAUCE

2 tablespoons sugar
3 tablespoons rice wine vinegar
3 tablespoons orange juice
1½ tablespoons tomato purée
1 tablespoon cornflour (cornstarch)
   blended with 3 tablespoons
   water

Oil for deep-frying
1 slice root ginger
2 tablespoons vegetable oil
1 small onion, thinly sliced

5-6 portions with other dishes

THE MOST POPULAR sweet and sour fish meal in China is made from Yellow River carp, but carp contains too many bones for the average Westerner. Use instead a fillet of fish such as cod, halibut, haddock, sole or plaice.

Method: Cut fish into 5 x 4 cm (2 x 1½ in) pieces. Sprinkle them with salt. Cut the capsicum halves into pieces half the size of the fish and the pineapple into 4 cm (1½ in) wedges. Mix the ingredients for the batter adding sufficient milk to make it smooth. Dip the pieces of fish in the batter. Mix the sauce ingredients together until smooth; set aside.

Heat oil to a depth of 4 cm (1½ in) in a wok or deep-fryer over medium heat. Test heat by dropping in the piece of ginger — when hot it will sizzle. Add the fish, one piece at a time, and deep-fry for 2 minutes. Remove the fish with a slotted spoon and drain.

Heat vegetable oil in a separate wok or frying pan. When hot, add onion and stir-fry for 30 seconds. Pour in the sauce and stir until it thickens. Add the fish pieces, spreading them out evenly in the pan. Turn them over gently in the sauce and cook them over low heat for 2 minutes. Serve.

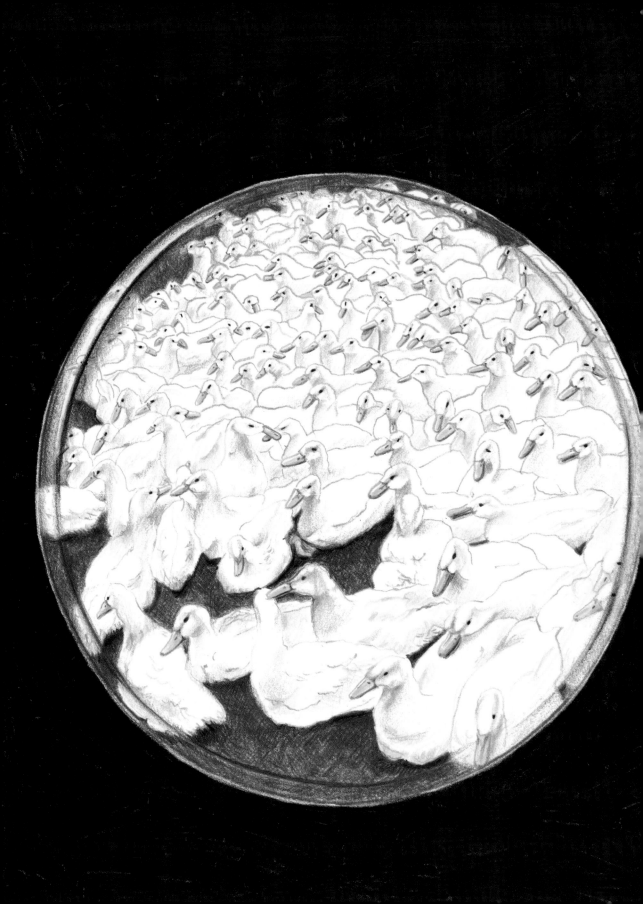

CHICKEN AND DUCK

CHICKEN AND DUCK

ONCE, CHICKEN WAS second to pork as the most widely used meat in Chinese cooking. In recent years it has overtaken pork in popularity, due to its cheap price and also availability. Like pork, chicken is both mild-tasting and savoury, and in Chinese cooking it is easily cooked and blended with other items of food to produce innumerable dishes.

Duck appears on the table less frequently than chicken, but it is easily the second most widely eaten fowl in China. The numerous streams, canals, rivers, lakes and water-ways of China produce great quantities of lively flocks of ducks every season, while an almost equal number of chickens peck around the farmyards in twos and threes. Because of its stronger flavour, duck is considered more special than chicken.

WHITE CUT CHICKEN

Bai Qie Ji

1.75-2 kg (3½-4 lb) young chicken
2.2 L (4 cups) water
4 slices root ginger
Salt to taste

SAUCE

3-4 tablespoons dark soya sauce
2 tablespoons rice wine vinegar
1½ teaspoons chilli sauce
2 tablespoons spring onions
*   (scallions), finely chopped*
3 cloves garlic, finely chopped
1 fresh chilli, seeded and finely
*   chopped*
2 teaspoons vegetable oil
1½ teaspoons sesame oil

5-8 portions

SERVE THIS AS a starter dish at a dinner party.

Method: Clean the chicken thoroughly. Bring water to the boil in a heavy saucepan. Add the ginger, salt and chicken to the boiling water. When contents return to a boil, lower the heat to a simmer and cook gently for 40 minutes, turning the chicken a couple of times. Turn the heat off, cover, and allow to cool completely in the stock.

To make the sauce, mix the ingredients in a bowl until well blended.

Serving: When the chicken is cool, remove from the stock. Reserve stock for some other purpose. Place chicken on a heavy chopping board and chop it into 5 x 4 cm (2 x 1½ in) pieces. Reassemble the pieces on a large serving dish roughly in the shape of a chicken. Pour the sauce evenly over the chicken and serve.

SHANGTUNG HAND-SHREDDED CHICKEN

Shan Dong Shou Si Ji

1 young roasting chicken weighing about 1.75-2 kg (3½-4 lb)
2 medium sticks of celery, chopped
4 slices root ginger, chopped
½ medium red capsicum (bell pepper), seeded and chopped
2 medium fresh chillies, seeded and chopped
4-5 thin slices of Sichuan pickles, chopped
3 spring onions (scallions), chopped
Salt to taste
3 cloves garlic, crushed

SAUCE

2 tablespoons light soya sauce
1 tablespoon rice wine vinegar
1½ tablespoons vegetable oil
1½ teaspoons sesame oil
2 tablespoons stock

6-10 portions with other dishes for a party

THIS TASTY DISH is easy to prepare and makes a good starter.

Method: Roast the chicken in an oven preheated to 200°C (400°F/Gas mark 6) for 1 hour, or until the juices run clear when the thigh is pricked with a fork. Let cool. Cut the chicken into small pieces and shred. Mix and toss together all the shredded chicken and vegetables on a serving platter. Sprinkle with salt and garlic. Mix all the ingredients for the sauce together until well blended.

Serving: Pour the sauce over the chicken and vegetables, and serve.

DRUNKEN CHICKEN

Zui Ji

*1 young chicken weighing about
    1.6 kg (3½ lb)*
1.8 L (6 cups) water
Salt to taste
2 medium onions, sliced
4-5 slices root ginger
*600 mL (2⅔ cups) rice wine or
    sherry*
*2 tablespoons spring onions
    (scallions), finely chopped*

8-10 portions with other dishes

IF SERVING AT a cocktail party as finger food, remove the bones or use boneless chicken breasts instead.

Method: Clean and truss the chicken. Bring water to the boil in a deep saucepan. Add salt, onions and ginger. Boil for 5 minutes. Add the chicken. Bring to the boil again. Reduce heat and simmer gently for 40 minutes. Let cool completely in the cooking liquid.

Drain completely. Place in a bowl. Pour in the rice wine or sherry. Turn chicken several times to ensure that it is covered evenly in wine. Cover and place in the refrigerator for 18 hours, turning every 6 hours.

Serving: Drain and untruss the chicken. Chop into 5 x 4 cm (2 x 1½ in) pieces. Arrange on a large serving plate, sprinkle with spring onions, and decorate by surrounding the chicken with flowers.

PAPER-WRAPPED CHICKEN

Zhi Bao Ji

4-5 medium dried black
  mushrooms
250 g (½ lb) boneless chicken
  breasts
3-4 broccoli spears
2 spring onions (scallions)
Edible rice paper or baking
  parchment
1 teaspoon vegetable oil
Salt to taste
Pepper to taste
1 teaspoon sugar
1 tablespoon light soya sauce
¾ tablespoon hoisin sauce
1 tablespoon rice wine or sherry
Oil for deep-frying

4-6 portions with other dishes

THIS IS AN ideal dish for a party or banquet.

Method: Soak dried mushrooms in hot water to cover for 30 minutes; drain. Remove the stems and cut caps into thin slices. Cut chicken into thin pieces. Blanch broccoli in boiling water for 2 minutes and break into individual florets. Cut spring onions diagonally into 4 cm (1½ in) sections. Cut rice paper or parchment into 15 x 10 cm (6 x 4 in) pieces. Rub the chicken with oil, sprinkle with salt, pepper and sugar, and let sit for 20 minutes. Add the vegetables and sprinkle with soya sauce, hoisin sauce and rice wine or sherry. Mix the vegetables with the chicken.

Use a large spoon to scoop up roughly 2 tablespoons of the chicken and vegetable mixture and place it just below the centre of a piece of paper. Fold the bottom edge up to cover the ingredients and turn the two sides in. Finally, fold the top edge down and tuck in. Press each envelope flat and pile them up as they are made.

In a wok or a deep, heavy pot, heat oil for deep-frying to a depth of 4 cm (1½ in). When very hot, carefully lower in 3 or 4 envelopes at a time. Fry for 2½-3 minutes. Remove and drain on absorbent paper.

Serving: When all the stuffed envelopes have been fried, arrange them on a heated plate. Open the steaming packages with the aid of chopsticks.

LEMON CHICKEN

Ning Meng Ji

*375 g (12 oz) boneless chicken
     breast*
Salt to taste
Pepper to taste
3 spring onions (scallions)
4 tablespoons vegetable oil
*3 slices root ginger, cut into double
     matchsticks*
*Rind of 1½ medium lemons, cut
     into double matchsticks*
*1 medium red capsicum (bell
     pepper), seeded and thinly sliced*
*1 medium green capsicum (bell
     pepper), seeded and thinly sliced*
3 tablespoons chicken stock
2 tablespoons rice wine or sherry
3 tablespoons light soya sauce
Juice from 2 medium lemons

4-5 portions with other dishes

THE SHARP, FRESH flavour of lemon is essential to the success of this — hence the late application of the lemon juice, which should not be cooked for any prolonged length of time.

Method: Cut chicken meat into 4 x 1 cm (1½ x ¼ in) slices. Rub chicken with 1 teaspoon oil and sprinkle with salt and pepper. Chop spring onions diagonally into 4 cm (1½ in) sections.

Heat the remaining oil in a wok or frying pan. When hot, add ginger, chicken and lemon rind. Stir-fry over high heat for 2 minutes. Remove and set aside.

Add spring onions and capsicums. Stir-fry over high heat. Pour in the stock, rice wine or sherry and soya sauce. When contents boil, return the chicken to the pan and toss in the sauce. After 1½ minutes, or when the liquid in the pan reduces by half, sprinkle with freshly squeezed lemon juice. Stir the contents once more over high heat and serve.

PEKING CHICKEN IN YELLOW BEAN SAUCE
Gong Bao Ji Ding

500 g (1 lb) boned chicken breasts
Salt to taste
1 egg white, lightly beaten
1½ tablespoons cornflour
  (cornstarch)
4 tablespoons cashew nuts

SAUCE

1½ tablespoons yellow bean sauce
1½ tablespoons dark soya sauce
1 tablespoon hoisin sauce
2 teaspoons sugar
¾ tablespoon cornflour (cornstarch)
  blended with 2 tablespoons
  water

3½ tablespoons vegetable oil
3 slices root ginger
1½ teaspoons sesame oil

5-6 portions with other dishes

THIS VERY TRADITIONAL Beijing (Peking) dish is
evocative of China's old capital.

Method: Dice chicken into 1.5 cm (½ in) cubes.
Sprinkle with salt, dip in egg white and dust with
cornflour. Heat the nuts in a dry pan, stir until crisp
and slightly brown, and set aside. To make the sauce,
mix all the ingredients until well blended.
  Heat the vegetable oil in a wok or frying pan.
Add the ginger and stir for 1 minute to flavour the
oil. Remove ginger with a slotted spoon. When the oil
is very hot, add the chicken cubes and spread them
evenly in the pan; shallow-fry for 1 minute. Turn the
chicken cubes over and shallow-fry for another
45 seconds. Push chicken to the side of the pan
away from the heat. Pour in the sauce and stir
over medium heat until the sauce thickens. Return
chicken cubes and stir-fry in the sauce over high heat
for 45 seconds. Add the crisp nuts and the sesame oil.
Continue to stir-fry for 30 seconds and serve.

CHICKEN IN VINEGAR SAUCE

Cu Liu Ji

315 g (10 oz) boned chicken breasts
90 g (3 oz) canned bamboo shoots
Salt to taste
1 egg white, lightly beaten
1 tablespoon cornflour (cornstarch)
4 tablespoons vegetable oil
1 medium onion, thinly sliced
1 clove garlic, chopped
2 slices root ginger, chopped
1 dried red chilli, chopped

SAUCE

1 tablespoon cornflour (cornstarch),
  blended with 3 tablespoons water
3 tablespoons rice wine vinegar
1½ tablespoons light soya sauce
1½ tablespoons chicken stock
1 tablespoon rice wine or sherry

4-6 portions with other dishes

THIS DISH IS enjoyed in Beijing (Peking) by people who appreciate the contrast of pronounced flavours. Here the sharp sour taste of the vinegar in the sauce is contrasted with the uncomplicated taste of the lightly salted chicken.

Method: Dice the chicken and bamboo shoots into 1.5 cm (½ in) cubes. Sprinkle chicken with salt, dip in egg white and dust with cornflour. To make sauce, mix all ingredients until well blended.

Heat 3 tablespoons of the vegetable oil in a wok or frying pan. When hot, add the diced chicken cubes and the bamboo shoots. Stir-fry over high heat for 2 minutes; remove from pan and set aside.

Add remaining 1 tablespoon oil to the pan. When hot, add onion, garlic, ginger and chilli. Stir over high heat for 1 minute. Pour in the sauce and stir until it thickens. Return the chicken and bamboo shoots to the pan. Stir-fry for 1 minute and serve.

RED-COOKED CHICKEN

Hong Shao Ji Jian

*1 chicken weighing about 2 kg
 (4 lb)*
4 tablespoons vegetable oil
2 medium onions, thinly sliced
4 slices root ginger, chopped
6-6½ tablespoons dark soya sauce
*6-6½ tablespoons rice wine or
 sherry*
*600 mL (2⅔ cups) chicken stock
 or water*
3 teaspoons sugar

6-8 portions

RED-COOKED DISHES ARE basic Chinese stews.
Meat and chicken, and in a some cases vegetables,
are stewed with soya sauce. This very simple form
of cooking is widely used in China. It produces large
quantities of delicious gravy to eat with boiled rice.

Method: Chop the chicken through the bones into
20-24 5 x 4 cm (2 x 1½ in) large bite-sized pieces.
   Heat oil in a heatproof casserole or heavy pot.
When hot, add onions and ginger and stir over
medium heat for 2 minutes. Add the chicken pieces
and turn in the hot oil for 3-4 minutes. Add soya
sauce, rice wine or sherry, stock or water and sugar.
Bring contents to a boil. Reduce heat to low and
simmer gently for 1 hour and 10 minutes, stirring
every 15 minutes. Add a little more water or stock
if the stew becomes too thick or dry.

Serving: Serve in a deep bowl accompanied with
ample quantities of boiled rice.

SHANGHAI SOYA-AND-GINGER-GLAZED CHICKEN

Shang Hai Jiang Jiang Ji

*1 chicken weighing about 2 kg
(4 lb)*
3 tablespoons vegetable oil
5 slices root ginger
2 medium onions, thinly sliced
5 tablespoons rice wine or sherry
1½ tablespoons sugar
3½ tablespoons dark soya sauce
2½ tablespoons yellow bean paste
2 tablespoons hoisin sauce
450 mL (2 cups) chicken stock

GARNISH

*1 spring onion (scallion), finely
chopped, or fresh coriander
(cilantro)*

6-8 portions with other dishes

QUICK STIR-BRAISING would be a good way to describe the process used for cooking this dish.

Method: Chop chicken through the bone into large bite-sized pieces. Cook in boiling water to cover for 5-6 minutes, then drain.

Heat oil in a large wok or a deep frying pan. Add ginger and onions. Stir-fry over medium heat for 3-4 minutes. Add the chicken pieces and all the remaining ingredients, except the garnish.
Raise the heat to high. The contents should soon boil and bubble.

Continue cooking on high heat for 18-20 minutes, turning the chicken as the stock reduces. The sauce should have now thickened to a glaze. Reduce the heat to prevent the sauce from burning. When the pieces of chicken begin to shine like glass, the coating has become more of a glaze than a sauce and the dish is ready to serve.

Serving: Garnish with a sprinkle of chopped spring onions or sprigs of coriander.

SALT-BURIED CRISPY CHICKEN
Yan Hong Ji

*1 young chicken weighing about
    2 kg (4 lb)*
2.5-3 kg (5-6 lb) coarse sea salt

8-10 portions with other dishes

THERE ARE MANY different recipes for Crispy Chicken in Chinese cuisine. This is probably the most interesting way to prepare it for a banquet.

Method: Rinse and dry the chicken thoroughly, cover loosely and refrigerate overnight. Heat salt in a deep heatproof casserole or pot over low heat for 10-15 minutes. When the salt is quite hot, form a depression and bury the chicken in it completely. Cover the pan and place it over low heat for 10 minutes. Transfer the pan to an oven preheated to 190°C (375°F/Gas mark 6) for 1½ hours.

Serving: Remove the chicken from the salt. When the salt is first brushed off the top of the chicken, the latter will appear surprisingly brown. Place it on a chopping board and chop it through the bone into 5 x 4 cm (2 x 1½ in) large bite-sized pieces. Pile them up on a well-heated serving plate and serve.
    Note: The salt may be used again.

PEKING DUCK

Beijing Kao Ya

2.5-2.75 kg (5-5½ lb) young duck

PANCAKES

500 g (1 lb) all-purpose flour
1½ teaspoons sugar
1 teaspoon oil
250 mL (1 cup) warm water
Sesame oil for brushing

SAUCE

3 tablespoons yellow bean paste
3 tablespoons sugar
2 tablespoons vegetable oil
2 teaspoons sesame oil

ALTERNATIVE SAUCE

2 tablespoons hoisin sauce
2 tablespoons plum sauce
1 tablespoon dark soya sauce
1 tablespoon vegetable oil
½ tablespoon sesame oil

10-12 spring onions (scallions) cut
*   into 5 cm (2 in) shreds*
1 medium cucumber, cut into
*   matchsticks*

6-8 portions

THE MOST FAMOUS duck dish in China is Peking Duck. Strangely enough, it is probably also one of the easiest to cook. Indeed, it is easier to cook in the average Western kitchen than in Beijing (Peking) itself. Peking Duck is a roast duck which has to be cooked in an oven, and since hardly any Chinese kitchen has an oven, therefore cannot be cooked at home. In Beijing, Peking Duck is only available in specialised restaurants (the top-line duck restaurants in Beijing prepare and serve nearly a thousand ducks a day), while in Europe, America and Australia, the dish can be prepared and cooked at home. The principal aim in preparing Peking Duck is to produce a duck with a distinctly crispy skin; this is carved off first and eaten together with thin slices of duck meat, which are wrapped in a pancake with shredded spring onions and cucumber, and doused with a sweet, fruity sauce. It is the combination of these contrasting flavours and textures which gives the dish its distinctive character and endows it with its enduring appeal.

Method: Rinse the duck inside and out and lower it into a large pan of boiling water for of 8-10 seconds. Drain well and wipe with several changes of paper towels to dry thoroughly. Cover loosely and refrigerate overnight. By the next day the skin of the bird should be sufficiently dry for it to be roasted in the oven.

   Preheat the oven to 200°C (400°F/Gas mark 6). Place duck on the top rack with a roasting pan underneath to catch any fluid. Roast for 1 hour, or until the duck is well cooked and the skin very crispy. Place spring onions and cucumber in small individual dishes for the diners to help themselves.

To make the pancakes, sift the flour into a mixing bowl. Stir in the sugar, oil and water with a pair of chopsticks or a wooden spoon until well mixed. Knead the mixture into a firm dough, then form it into 2 large "sausage" strips. Cut each strip into 10 or 12 pieces and form each piece into a small ball. Flatten each ball into a round disc. Brush the top of one of the discs with sesame oil, and place a second disc on top to form a sandwich. Using a small rolling pin, roll the sandwich into a pancake of about 15 cm (6 in) in diameter. Repeat until you have used up all the dough balls and made them into sandwich pancakes.

Heat a dry frying pan over low/medium heat. When hot, place a sandwich pancake on the pan and shake so that the pancake doesn't stick to the surface of the pan. After 1½ minutes turn the pancake over and cook the other side until the pancake begins to puff and bubble slightly. The pancake is ready when some brown spots begin to appear on the underside. Now very gently peel the sandwich apart into its two separate pancakes. Fold each pancake in half and stack them up. If they are not to be used immediately, cover with a damp cloth. They can be reheated in a steamer for a couple of minutes, if necessary.

To make either sauce, combine all ingredients in a small pan and stir over low heat until smooth.

Serving: Cut the skin of the duck into 4-5 cm (1½-2 in) slices with a sharp knife and serve on a heated dish. Slice the meat off the duck into similar-sized pieces and serve on a separate heated dish.

Diners help themselves by spreading sauce lavishly over the duck skin and meat, sandwiched inside a pancake with shredded spring onions and cucumber.

CRISPY AND AROMATIC DUCK
Xiang Cui Ya

2 kg (4 lb) duck
Salt to taste
Freshly ground pepper to taste
¾ teaspoon five spice powder
5 slices root ginger, shredded
5 spring onions (scallions),
    shredded
4 cloves garlic, shredded

MARINADE

3 tablespoons light soya sauce
2 tablespoons rice wine vinegar
1½ tablespoons honey

6-8 portions with other dishes

CRISPY AND AROMATIC DUCK is similar to Peking Duck. The cooking method, however, differs: First the duck is steamed, then deep-fried, so that its skin is crispier than that of Peking Duck.

Method: Rinse and dry the duck thoroughly, inside and out. Combine the salt, pepper and five spice powder. Rub the mixture over the duck, then sprinkle with ginger, spring onions and garlic. Leave the duck to season for 2 hours.

To make the marinade, combine all the ingredients and rub evenly over the duck. Wrap the duck in aluminium foil and place it in a refrigerator to marinate overnight.

After marinating overnight the duck is ready to be cooked, first by steaming, then by deep-frying. The long period of steaming cooks the meat and steams away any excess fat and seasoning; the short period of deep-frying crisps the outer skin.

To steam the duck, remove the foil, place the duck in a steamer and cook for 50-55 minutes. Remove from the steamer and let cool.

When cool, double deep-fry the duck for a total of 10-11 minutes; that is, deep-fry twice for 5-6 minutes each, with a break of about 5 minutes between the two sessions of deep-frying.

Serving: To serve this dish, pull the meat and skin of the duck off the bones. Diners help themselves by wrapping duck in pancakes with shredded vegetables, and liberally spreading with a piquant sauce. (For the pancake and sauce recipes, see Peking Duck on page 116.)

CANTONESE ROAST DUCK

Shao Ya

2-2.5 kg (4-5 lb) duck
Salt to taste
2 tablespoons vegetable oil
3 tablespoons chopped onion
2 spring onions (scallions), chopped
    diagonally into 2.5 cm (1 in)
    pieces
3 tablespoons chopped parsley
2 cloves garlic, crushed
1½ teaspoons crushed peppercorns
150 mL (⅔ cup) chicken stock
3 tablespoons light soya sauce
2 tablespoons rice wine or sherry
1 tablespoon sugar
½ teaspoon five spice powder
2 tablespoons honey
1½ tablespoons rice wine vinegar
150 mL (⅔ cup) boiling water
1½ teaspoons cornflour
    (cornstarch) blended with 2
    tablespoons water

5-6 portions with other dishes

THIS IS THE DUCK which is most often seen hanging in Chinese restaurants or shop windows.

Method: Rinse the duck under running water and dry thoroughly. Tie the neck tightly with string, so that no liquid will drip out. Let sit uncovered for 2 hours, then rub it generously inside and out with salt.

Heat oil in a small saucepan. Add chopped onion, spring onions, parsley, garlic and peppercorns. Stir-fry for 2 minutes. Pour in the stock. Bring to a boil and simmer gently for 5-6 minutes. Add soya sauce, rice wine or sherry, sugar and five spice powder, and blend well. Pour this mixture inside the duck and close the cavity tightly with skewers and string so no liquid leaks out. In a separate bowl mix honey and vinegar with boiling water to use for basting the duck.

Preheat the oven to 200°C (400°F/Gas mark 6). Roast the duck on a rack (or hang the duck inside the oven tailside up) for 15 minutes. Baste the duck with the honey-vinegar mixture. Place the bird back in the oven to roast at the reduced heat of 190°C (375°F/Gas mark 5) for 1 hour, basting at 30-minute intervals. After the second basting, roast the duck for 30 minutes.

Remove the bird from the oven to cool for a minute or two. Then carefully remove the strings and skewers, and pour the liquid from the bird's cavity into a pan. Stir in the blended cornflour and stir over medium heat until thickened.

Serving: Cut the duck into smaller pieces and place on a serving plate. Pour the sauce over and serve hot. As this dish is rich, it is best served with rice and plain cooked vegetables.

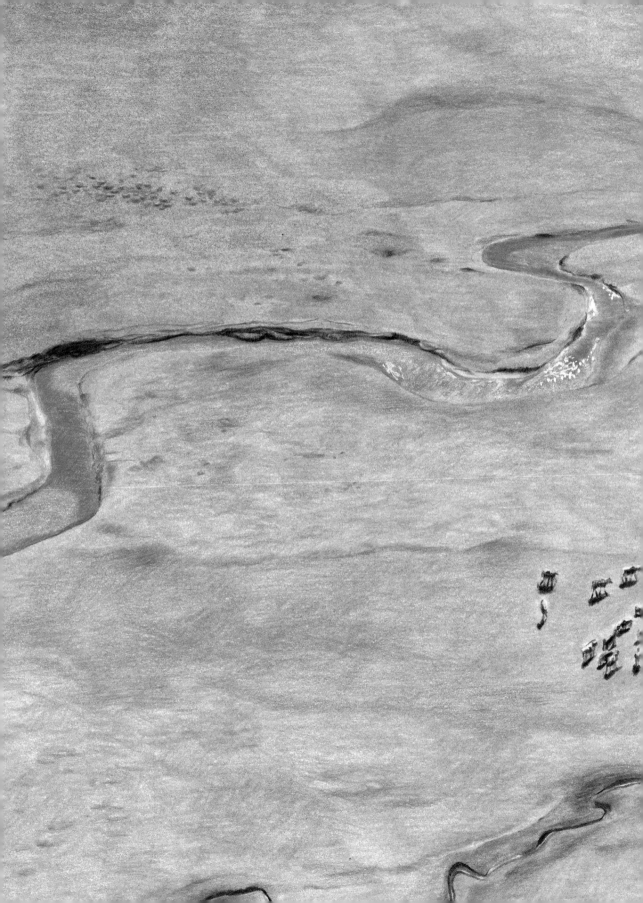

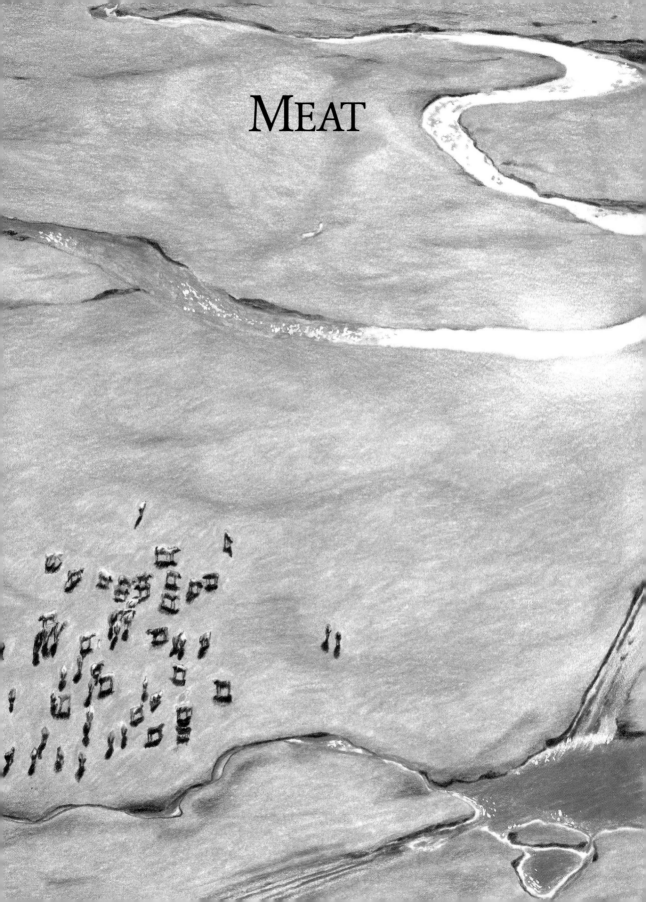

MEAT

MEAT

PORK IS THE most versatile and widely used meat in China. We Chinese do not have as great a preference for lean meat as you have in the West. Indeed, the favourite cut of pork in China is Five Flower Pork or pork belly (fresh bacon or side pork), which consists of skin and alternating layers of lean pork and fat. Although Westerners are horrified by the cholesterol levels of such cuts, we Chinese eat so little meat that it isn't a problem.

Pork skin plays an important part in Chinese cooking. It is used in boiled and stewed dishes to thicken the stock or gravy, so that thickening agents (cornflour/cornstarch, potato flour, etc.) aren't necessary. This results in a very tasty sauce which is useful for adding to rice and noodles and for coating and flavouring vegetables.

Beef makes only an occasional appearance on the Chinese dining table, probably because cattle in China are raised as work animals rather than as a food source. In the areas south of the Yangzi (Yangtze) River, lamb is seldom eaten at all as it is considered a kind of game meat which is not to the taste of the southern palates.

However, to the north nearer the steppes of the great grasslands of Mongolia and western Manchuria, large herds of cattle roam. Here lamb and beef are the principal meats. Lamb is popular as it doesn't require the lengthy cooking that tougher beef needs. Indeed, Beijing (Peking) was once known as "Mutton City", because many of its best-known and most popular dishes contained lamb.

Many Chinese beef and lamb dishes have a Muslim/ Mongolian background. With improved communication in China, the Chinese Muslim minorities have become more dispersed. Beef and lamb dishes can now be eaten in Chinese Muslim restaurants in any principal city of China.

WHITE-CUT GARLIC PORK

Bai Qiu Rou

*1.25-1.5 kg (2½-3 lb) pork belly
    (fresh bacon or side pork) cut to
    include several layers of lean
    and fat, in addition to a good
    layer of skin at the top*
4-5 slices root ginger
Salt to taste
2.2-2.8 L (4-5 pt) water

DIPPING SAUCE

5-6 cloves garlic, crushed
3 tablespoons light soya sauce
4 tablespoons rice wine vinegar

4-6 portions with other dishes

THIS NORTHERN DISH is a good introductory course to a meal with a number of elaborately flavoured dishes. The uncomplicated flavours of the pork and rice make this an appealing dish.

Method: Place pork in a deep saucepan. Add ginger, salt and enough water to cover the pork. Bring contents to the boil and boil for 10 minutes. Pour away one-third of the water. Reduce heat to a slow simmer and simmer gently for 35 minutes, turning the pork over every 10 minutes.

To make the dipping sauce, combine ingredients in a bowl and divide between 2 small dishes on the table.

Serving: Remove the pork from the pan and allow it to cool. When cold, cut the pork through the skin and the layers of lean and fat into slices 4 x 6 cm (1½-2½ in). Overlap them neatly on a serving plate. Each tender slice of pork should be first dipped into the sauce before it is eaten with hot rice.

BASIC RED-COOKED PORK

Hong Shao Rou

1.5-2 kg (3-4 lb) pork belly (fresh bacon or side pork)
3-4 slices root ginger
5-6 tablespoons dark soya sauce
3 teaspoons sugar

6-7 portions with other dishes

THIS PARTICULAR RECIPE is probably the most widely cooked meat dish in China. No doubt it is popular because it is easy to cook and is delicious with rice, noodles, steamed bread and vegetables. The jelly-like tenderness of the meat and tastiness of the gravy make this dish particularly appealing.

Method: Cut pork into 6 x 4 cm (2½ x 1½ in) crosswise slices 1.5 cm (½ in) thick, with each slice including skin and layers of lean meat and fat. Place the pork pieces in a pan of boiling water to boil for 5 minutes. Pour away three-quarters of the water, leaving enough to cover all the pork pieces.

Add ginger, soya sauce and sugar to the pan, sprinkling them evenly over the pork. Cover the pan tightly and bring to the boil. Lower the heat to the minimum and simmer as gently as possible for 1 hour and 15 minutes, stirring the meat every 15 minutes and replenishing with 5-6 tablespoons of boiling water whenever the contents appear too dry.

The pork may also be placed in a heatproof casserole, placed in an oven preheated to 195°C (390°F/Gas mark 6) and cooked for the same length of time, stirring the meat 3 times during the course of the cooking.

Serving: Transfer the pork from the pan to a serving plate or bring the casserole to the table for the diners to help themselves.

Note: Basic Red-Cooked Pork can become Red-Cooked Pork with Bamboo Shoots or Red-Cooked Pork with Water Chestnuts simply by adding either of those ingredients to the pan or casserole during the last 30 minutes of cooking.

RED-COOKED PORK WITH SPINACH

Hong Shao Zhu Shou

2 kg (4 lb) pork knuckle (hock)
Salt to taste
4-5 tablespoons dark soya sauce
2 spring onions (scallions)
3 cloves garlic, crushed
3 slices root ginger
5 tablespoons vegetable oil
500 g (1 lb) fresh spinach
1 tablespoon sugar
3 tablespoon rice wine or sherry
2 teaspoons fermented beancurd
*   (tofu) (optional)*

6-8 portions for a small party or
*   family gathering with other*
*   dishes*

THIS IS SIMILAR to *Eisbein*, the beloved dish of the Germans and northern Europeans, except that the Europeans do not use soya sauce. The addition of soya sauce to the pork transforms the dish.

Method: Clean the skin of the pork, removing any hair. Cut the knuckle-end halfway lengthwise and remove the bone (or ask the butcher to do it). Rub the pork with salt and 2 tablespoons soya sauce. Cut spring onions diagonally into 2.5 cm (1 in) sections and combine with garlic and ginger. Mix them all in a bowl with half of the remaining soya sauce.

Heat oil in a wok or frying pan. Add knuckle and fry for 7-8 minutes until slightly brown. Stuff the cavity of the knuckle with the shallots, garlic, ginger and soya sauce. Wash spinach thoroughly and drain. Remove the stems of the spinach.

Choose a deep casserole or heavy pot with a lid. Place the stuffed knuckle in it sitting vertically. Sprinkle with sugar, rice wine or sherry and the remaining 2 to 3 tablespoons soya sauce, and add the fermented beancurd. Pour in water to cover the knuckle. Bring contents to the boil and then transfer the casserole to an oven preheated to 200°C (400°F/ Gas mark 6). After 15 minutes reduce heat to 180°C (350°F/Gas mark 4) and simmer very gently for 2½ hours, turning the knuckle over every 30 minutes. Lift the knuckle out to stand vertically at the centre of a large serving dish. Add the spinach to the casserole and cook over high heat for 6-7 minutes. Ladle out the sauce to surround the knuckle and pour any remaining gravy in the casserole over the top.

LION'S HEAD MEATBALLS

Shi Zi Tou

4 medium dried black mushrooms
100 g (4 oz) bean thread
 (transparent) noodles
1.25 kg (2½ lb) pork belly (fresh
 bacon or side pork), including
 lean meat, fat and skin
2 medium onions
4-5 medium canned water
 chestnuts
Salt to taste
Pepper to taste
4 tablespoons dark soya sauce
1½ teaspoons sugar
½ egg white, lightly beaten
Oil for deep-frying
300 mL (1⅓ cups) beef stock
2 spring onions (scallions), chopped

6 portions with other dishes

LION'S HEAD MEATBALLS is a festive dish, so-called because the golden-brown noodles in the sauce resemble the mane of a lion. The meatballs are cooked for a long time to achieve succulence and tenderness.

Method: Soak dried mushrooms in hot water for 30 minutes. Discard stems and chop caps finely. Soak noodles in hot water for 15 minutes and drain.

  Coarsely chop the pork with a cleaver or blender. Coarsely chop onions and water chestnuts. Place them in a bowl with salt, pepper, 2 tablespoons soya sauce, sugar and egg white. Mix together until well blended. Form into 5-6 large meatballs. Wet your fingers and palms first so that the chopped meat will not stick to them.

  Heat oil to a depth of 7½ cm (3 in) in a wok or deep-fryer. When hot, add 2 meatballs at a time to fry lightly for 5 minutes or until slightly brown and firm. Remove and arrange the meatballs in the bottom of a saucepan or heatproof bowl with a lid suitable for putting in a steamer for lengthy steaming. Sprinkle the top of each meatball with 1 teaspoon of the remaining soya sauce. Insert the pan or bowl into a steamer and steam steadily for 2½ hours.

Serving: Remove and transfer the meatballs to a serving bowl. Pour the remaining liquid from the pan or bowl into a saucepan. Add stock and chopped dried mushrooms, adjust for seasoning, and bring to a boil for 5 minutes. Add the noodles to simmer together until tender. Pour all the contents over the meatballs in the serving dish. Sprinkle with chopped spring onions and serve.

TWICE-COOKED PORK

Hui Guo Rou

1 kg (2¼ lb) pork belly (fresh bacon
   or side pork)
1 red capsicum (bell pepper)
1 green capsicum (bell pepper)

SAUCE

1½ tablespoons yellow bean paste
2 tablespoons dark soya sauce
2 tablespoons tomato purée
1½ tablespoons hoisin sauce
2 teaspoons chilli sauce
2 tablespoons chicken stock

4 tablespoons vegetable oil
3 cloves garlic, chopped
60 g (2 oz) Sichuan pickles,
   chopped
2 fresh chillies, seeded and chopped
2 tablespoons rice wine or sherry
1½ tablespoons spring onions
   (scallions)
1 teaspoon sesame oil

5-6 portions with other dishes

THIS IS A SPICY dish, typical of Sichuan food.

Method: Boil pork in water to cover for 35 minutes.
When cold, drain and cut into 6 x 4 cm (2½ x 1½ in)
lean-and-fat slices about 1 cm (¼ in) thick. Cut
capsicums into 4 cm (1½ in) strips. To make the
sauce, mix the ingredients until well blended.

Heat the oil in a wok or frying pan. When hot, add
the garlic, pickles and chillies, and stir them in the
hot oil for 30 seconds. Pour in the sauce and heat
until it bubbles over high heat. Add the sliced pork
and stir. Continue to stir-fry over high heat for 2 full
minutes. Sprinkle with sherry, spring onions and
sesame oil, stir and serve.

PORK SPARE-RIBS

Men Kao Pai Gu

1.75-2 kg (3½-4 lb) pork spare-ribs
Salt to taste
Pepper to taste

MARINADE

2 tablespoons salted black beans
2 tablespoons light soya sauce
1 tablespoon yellow bean paste
4 slices root ginger, finely chopped
3 cloves garlic, crushed
1 medium onion, sliced
1 tablespoon sugar
3 tablespoons dry sherry
2 tablespoons vegetable oil

600 mL (2 cups) strong chicken
   stock

5-6 portions

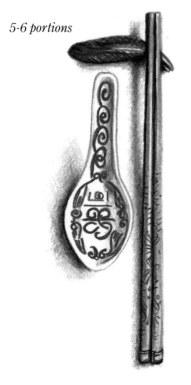

SPARE-RIBS HAVE now become a universally popular dish that probably originated in China. One of the first jobs in cooking spare-ribs is to render the meat sufficiently tender so that it can be easily detached from the bone. This tenderising process is achieved by stewing or steaming. If they are steamed, the ribs need to be marinated in advance. The flavour can be further enhanced by next crisping the spare-ribs for a short period by deep-frying or roasting in a hot oven.

In the average Western kitchen the simplest way to cook spare-ribs is to stew them first, then crisp them in a hot oven.

Method: Cut spare-ribs into individual ribs. Sprinkle them evenly with salt and pepper to taste. Chop and mash the black beans. Mix all the ingredients for the marinade in a large bowl. Add the spare-ribs. Turn and rub the ribs with the marinade several times until every rib is well coated. Let stand for 30 minutes.

Heat stock in a large casserole. Add the ribs to the boiling stock. Pour in any remaining marinade. Cover the casserole, reduce heat and simmer for 30-35 minutes, turning the ribs every 10-12 minutes. Remove the lid from the casserole and place in an oven preheated to 200°C (400°F/Gas mark 6). Roast for approximately 10-12 minutes or until the ribs are crisp.

Serving: Bring the casserole to the table for the diners to help themselves. As spare-ribs are an informal dish, diners are encouraged to use their fingers.

SWEET AND SOUR PORK

Gu Lu Rou

500 g (1 lb) leg of pork (fresh ham)
Salt to taste
½ egg white, lightly beaten
2 tablespoons cornflour (cornstarch)
1 red capsicum (bell pepper)

SAUCE

1 tablespoon cornflour (cornstarch)
2 tablespoons water
3½ tablespoons rice wine vinegar
1 tablespoon light soya sauce
1½ tablespoons sugar
2 tablespoons orange juice
1 tablespoon tomato purée

5 tablespoons vegetable oil
1 medium onion, thinly sliced
1 slice pineapple, cubed

6-7 portions with other dishes

THE APPEAL OF this dish, which is similar to that of the French dish Duck à l'Orange, is the way it sets off the richness of the meat with the freshness of the slightly sharp, fruity sauce.

Method: Cut pork into thick slices and then roughly into 4 x 2.5 cm (1½ x 1 in) pieces. Sprinkle with salt, dip in egg white and dust with cornflour. Cut capsicum into 4 cm (1½ in) strips. To make the sauce, mix the ingredients together until well blended.

Heat oil in a wok or a frying pan. When hot, add the pork pieces and stir-fry over medium heat for 3 minutes. Remove them with a slotted spoon and set aside.

Drain away half of the remaining oil. Add the onion and stir-fry for 1 minute. Add the pineapple and capsicum. Continue to stir-fry for another minute. Pour in the sauce and stir until the sauce thickens. Return the pork pieces to the wok and mix with the sauce over medium heat for 1½ minutes, or until every piece of pork appears glistening and well coated with the sauce. Serve with rice.

CANTONESE BARBECUED PORK

Chao Shao

1 kg (2 lb) fillet of pork (tenderloin)

MARINADE

3 tablespoons dark soya sauce
1½ tablespoons hoisin sauce
1½ tablespoons yellow bean paste
1 tablespoon sugar
1½ tablespoons tomato purée
1 tablespoon rice wine or sherry
1 tablespoon vegetable oil

6-7 portions with other dishes

THE APPEAL OF this dish lies in the spicy coating that surrounds each piece of pork, while inside the meat is very moist and juicy. It can be eaten hot or cold. When served cold, it can be used as an appetizer.

Method: Trim the pork thoroughly, removing any fat or membrane. To make the marinade, mix all the ingredients together until well blended and pour over the entire fillet of pork, rubbing it into the meat thoroughly. Leave pork to stand in the marinade for 2 hours, basting and turning the meat over every 30 minutes.

Preheat the oven to 200°C (400°F/Gas mark 6). Place the pork in a roasting pan and bake for 20-25 minutes, turning the pork after the first 10 minutes. Let cool slightly. Cut the pork across the grain into 1 cm (¼ in) thick slices.

Serving: Serve the pork by overlapping the slices on a serving plate.

RED-COOKED FIVE SPICE BEEF WITH TURNIPS

Luo Bo Men Niu Nan

1.25 kg (2½ lb) beef shin (shank)
500 g (1 lb) turnips
3½ tablespoons vegetable oil
2 medium onions, thinly sliced
3 slices root ginger, shredded
¾ teaspoon five spice powder
Salt to taste
900 mL (4 cups) water
3½ tablespoons dark soya sauce
2 teaspoons sugar
6 tablespoons rice wine or sherry

6-7 portions with other dishes

THIS VERY TASTY dish is excellent to consume on a cold wintry day!

Method: Boil beef in water to cover for 10 minutes, then drain and cut into 4 x 2.5 cm (1½ x 1 in) cubes. Clean and cut turnips diagonally into 4 cm (1½ in) pieces.

Heat oil in a heatproof casserole or heavy pot. When hot, add beef and stir-fry the beef cubes for 3-4 minutes. Remove with a slotted spoon and set aside. Add onions, ginger, five spice and salt. Stir-fry for 3-4 minutes. Pour in water. Add soya sauce, sugar, rice wine or sherry. Bring contents to the boil. Add the beef cubes. When contents return to the boil, reduce heat to a minimum, cover and simmer very gently for 1½ hours. Add the turnips and stir the mixture several times. Add 300 mL (1⅓ cups) of water if the contents begin to run too dry. Stir the mixture again. Cover the casserole and place in an oven preheated to 195°C (390°F/Gas mark 6) for 1¾ hours.

Serving: Bring the casserole to the table. Remove the lid and allow diners to help themselves, spooning the beef, turnips and gravy into their own bowl with rice.

RED-COOKED LAMB WITH CARROTS AND DRIED TANGERINE PEEL

Chen Pi Yang Rou

1.25 kg (2½ lb) leg of lamb
500 g (1 lb) carrots
3½ tablespoons vegetable oil
2 medium onions
3 slices root ginger
3 cloves garlic, crushed
2½ tablespoons dried tangerine
    peel, in small pieces
Salt to taste
900 mL (4 cups) water
3½ teaspoons dark soya sauce
1 teaspoon sugar
6 tablespoons rice wine or sherry

6-7 portions with other dishes

THIS LAMB DISH is very similar to Red-Cooked
Five Spice Beef with Turnips, except that here, the
turnips are replaced by carrots, and the five spice
powder by dried tangerine peel, which is used
frequently for flavouring in long-cooked meat dishes.
Since leg of lamb can be tenderised much more
quickly than beef shin, the overall cooking time
can be shortened by 1 hour.

Method: Boil the lamb in water to cover. Drain and
cut into 4 x 2.5 cm (1½ x 1 in) cubes. Clean and cut
the carrots diagonally into 4 cm (1½ in) sections.
   Heat oil in a heatproof casserole or heavy pot.
When hot, add lamb and stir-fry for 3-4 minutes.
Remove with a slotted spoon and set aside.
Add onions, ginger, garlic, tangerine peel and salt.
Stir-fry for 3-4 minutes. Pour in water and add soya
sauce, sugar, and rice wine or sherry. Bring to a boil
and add the lamb cubes. Reduce heat to low, cover
and simmer gently for 1 hour. Add the carrots.
Stir contents and cover. Place in the oven preheated
to 195°C (390°F/Gas mark 6) for 1 hour. It is then
ready to serve.

SLICED BEEF IN SOFT SCRAMBLED EGGS

Niu Rou Chao Dan

500 g (1 lb) fillet of beef
(tenderloin)

MARINADE

1½ tablespoons dark soya sauce
½ tablespoon yellow bean paste
½ tablespoon hoisin sauce
1 teaspoon chilli sauce

Salt to taste
Pepper to taste
3 eggs, beaten
1 tablespoon spring onions
(scallions)
½ tablespoon hoisin sauce
3 tablespoons vegetable oil
1 tablespoon rice wine or sherry

4-5 portions with other dishes

THE AROMA OF wine combines well with the taste of eggs, giving this dish an interesting flavour.

Method: Cut beef into very thin slices 5 x 4 cm (2 x 1½ in) in size. Place them in a bowl. Mix all the marinade ingredients together until well blended. Add the marinade to the beef and rub it into every individual slice of beef. Let sit for 30 minutes. Add salt and pepper to beaten eggs along with chopped spring onions, hoisin sauce and 1 tablespoon of oil. Beat again for another 15 seconds.

Heat 1 tablespoon oil in a wok or frying pan over medium heat. When hot, add the sliced beef in a single layer to cook for 45 seconds. Stir-fry for another 30 seconds. Remove and set aside. Add the remaining 1 tablespoon of oil. Tilt the pan so that the oil evenly covers the surface. Pour in the beaten eggs. When they are half set and still wet on the top, add the slices of beef and stir-fry together with the eggs. Sprinkle with rice wine or sherry and stir over medium heat until eggs are just set.

Serving: This is an excellent dish to eat hot with plain rice.

COLD-TOSSED BEEF IN MUSTARD SAUCE WITH FRESH CORIANDER

Liang Ban Niu Rou

*700 g (1½ lb) beef fillet
    (tenderloin) or rump (sirloin)*
1 tablespoon vegetable oil
Salt to taste
Pepper to taste
*1 small bunch fresh coriander
    (cilantro), washed*
1½ tablespoons rice wine or sherry

SAUCE

3 teaspoons hot mustard
1½ tablespoons light soya sauce
1 tablespoon rice wine vinegar
1½ tablespoons beef stock
1 tablespoon sesame oil

8-12 portions as a starter

THIS IS A VERY useful dish to serve as an appetizer.

Method: Boil beef in water to cover for 15 minutes. When cold, cut into very thin slices approximately 6 x 2.5 cm (2½ x 1 in) in size. Rub beef with oil and sprinkle with salt and pepper. To make the sauce, mix the ingredients together until well blended.

Serving: Stir the beef and the sauce together in a large deep-sided serving bowl. Strew the top with coriander sprigs and sprinkle with rice wine or sherry. Stir once more and serve.

SICHUAN SHREDDED BEEF WITH CARROTS AND CELERY

Si Chuan Niu Rou Si

500 g (1 lb) rump steak (sirloin)
Salt to taste
4 tablespoons cornflour
    (cornstarch)
1 egg, beaten
2 slices root ginger
2 medium carrots
2-3 sticks celery
Oil for deep-frying
2 tablespoons beef stock

SAUCE

1½ tablespoons cornflour
    (cornstarch), blended with 3
    tablespoons water
1 tablespoon light soya sauce
1 tablespoon sugar
2 tablespoons rice wine vinegar
2 tablespoons rice wine or sherry
¾ tablespoon Sichuan hot bean
    paste

6-8 portions with other dishes

THE HOT SPICINESS of the sweet and sour sauce here gives this dish its typical Sichuan character and appeal.

Method: Cut the beef into double matchsticks. Sprinkle with salt. Mix cornflour with beaten egg to make a smooth batter. Coat beef with a layer of batter. Clean and cut ginger, carrots and celery into the same size matchsticks as the beef. To make the sauce, mix the ingredients together until well blended.

Heat the oil in a wok or frying pan over medium heat. When hot (a crumb will sizzle when dropped into it), add the beef slowly, in small quantities. Use a fork or a pair of chopsticks to keep the pieces of beef apart, so that they will fry singly rather than in large clusters. Continue to stir with the chopsticks. After 3-3½ minutes, remove and drain the beef and set aside. Pour away most of the oil.

Add the carrots, celery and ginger and stir for 1 minute. Add stock and stir once more. Pour in the sauce. Turn the heat to high. When the contents begin to boil, return the beef to the wok and stir in the sauce with the vegetables. Stir-fry for 1 minute and serve.

BEEF IN OYSTER SAUCE WITH SNOW PEAS

He Dou Niu Rou

500 g (1 lb) lean beef steak
Salt to taste
Pepper to taste
1 egg white, lightly beaten
2 tablespoons cornflour
(cornstarch)
120-150 g (4-5 oz) snow peas
(mange tout)
4 tablespoons vegetable oil
2 slices root ginger, coarsely
chopped
2¼ tablespoons oyster sauce
3 tablespoons beef stock
1½ tablespoons rice wine or sherry
1½ tablespoons dark soya sauce

5-6 portions with other dishes

THIS IS A TYPICAL Cantonese dish with an interesting blend of beef and oyster flavours. Normally served with rice, it may also be served as a savoury starter.

Method: Cut beef into thin slices 5 x 4 cm (2 x 1½ in) in size. Sprinkle with salt and pepper to taste, dip in egg white and dust with cornflour. Blanch snow peas in boiling water for 1 minute and drain.

Heat oil in a wok or frying pan. When hot, add the ginger to flavour the oil, and add the beef, spreading it out over the surface of the pan. Add half of the oyster sauce to the beef, stir-fry for 1 minute; remove and set aside. Add the snow peas to the pan, then the stock and rice wine or sherry. Turn the heat to high and stir-fry the vegetables for 1 minute. Return the beef to the pan, sprinkle the contents with the soya sauce and the remaining oyster sauce, stir-fry the contents for a further 1 minute and serve.

BEEF IN BLACK BEAN SAUCE WITH CAPSICUMS

Chi Jiao Niu Rou

500 g (1 lb) rump steak (sirloin)
1 egg white, lightly beaten
2 tablespoons cornflour
*   (cornstarch)*
2 medium green or red capsicums
*   (bell peppers), seeded*
1½ tablespoons salted black beans
3 tablespoons vegetable oil
1 tablespoon dark soya sauce
1 tablespoon beef stock
1 tablespoon rice wine or sherry
½ tablespoon Sichuan hot bean
*   paste*

5 portions with other dishes

THIS DISH should be served with ample rice.

Method: Cut beef into thin slices 5 x 2.5 cm (2 x 1 in) in size. Dip in egg white and dust with cornflour. Cut capsicums into 5 x 2.5 cm (2 x 1 in) strips. Soak black beans in hot water for 20 minutes, then drain, leaving 1½ tablespoons water with the beans.

   Heat oil in a wok or frying pan. When hot, add the beef and stir-fry over medium heat for 1¼ minutes. Remove beef and set aside. Add black beans with water and mash with the oil in the pan. Return the beef to the pan to coat with a layer of the sauce. Add soya sauce, stock, rice wine or sherry, hot bean paste and the capsicums. Stir-fry together for 1 minute over high heat and serve.

PEPPERED BEEF WITH ONION

Hei Jiao Niu Liu

*500 g (1 lb) fillet of beef
    (tenderloin)*
Salt to taste
Pepper to taste
1 egg white, lightly beaten
*2 tablespoons cornflour
    (cornstarch)*
5 tablespoons vegetable oil
*2 slices root ginger, coarsely
    chopped*
1 teaspoon Sichuan peppercorns
2 medium onions, thinly sliced
1½ teaspoons sugar
2 tablespoons dark soya sauce

5-6 portions with other dishes

THE PEPPERED BEEF in this dish is popular in the West.

Method: Cut beef into thin slices 5 x 4 cm (2 x 1½ in) in size. Sprinkle with salt and a generous amount of pepper, dip in egg white and dust with cornflour.

Heat 4 tablespoons oil in wok or frying pan over medium heat. When hot, add ginger and peppercorns. Stir-fry for 45 seconds. Add the beef, spreading it out over the surface of the pan, and stir-fry for 1 minute over high heat. Remove and set aside.

Add remaining 1 tablespoon oil, and when hot, add the sliced onions. Stir-fry for 1½ minutes. Add sugar and soya sauce, return the beef, and continue to stir-fry all the ingredients for 1½ minutes over high heat. Serve.

Serving: This is a dish which should be served hot with rice.

MONGOLIAN HOT POT

Shuan Yang Rou

DIPPING SAUCES; *the following mixture of ingredients may be tried*

SAUCE 1
slices of root ginger, shredded
3 tablespoons light soya sauce
5 tablespoons rice wine vinegar
1 tablespoon vegetable oil

SAUCE 2
5 cloves garlic, crushed
3 tablespoons light soya sauce
2 tablespoons rice wine vinegar
2 tablespoons rice wine or sherry
1 tablespoon sesame oil

SAUCE 3
3 spring onions (scallions), coarsely chopped
3 tablespoons light soya sauce
2 tablespoons tomato sauce
1½ tablespoons Sichuan hot bean paste
1 tablespoon sesame oil

SAUCE 4
3 tablespoons chopped fresh coriander (cilantro)
1½ tablespoons hot mustard
2 tablespoons light soya sauce
2 tablespoons chicken stock
1 tablespoon vegetable oil
1½ tablespoons rice wine or sherry
1 tablespoon sesame oil

THIS DISH, ONE of the best-known culinary features of Beijing (Peking), was first introduced from Mongolia in 1855 during the reign of Emperor Shanfeng of the Qing Dynasty. Traditionally only lamb was used, but as the dish became popular further south, other types of meat, such as chicken, beef and pork, were added. Later, even fish and seafood were cooked in this way.

The original recipe was several thousand words long, and a whole chapter of a book was needed to describe the preparation, cooking and consumption of the dish. Yet, in reality, it is such a simple dish that it should not take more than half a postcard to describe and present. Here, I shall describe and present it as simply and concisely as I can.

Having had this dish scores of times during the five years I spent in Beijing, I would say that the dish consists of nothing more than a leg of lamb cut into extremely thin slices. The slices are then spread out on serving dishes in single layers for diners to help themselves. There should be at least two dishfuls of lamb for each diner.

The dish is sometimes called *fondue chinoise*. As with Swiss fondue the diners actually do the cooking at the dining table. In Beijing, the cooking is usually done in a hotpot fired by charcoal. In the West it can be done in any deep, heavy pot in which the heat can be easily controlled.

The cooking consists of dipping the extremely thinly-sliced lamb in the boiling broth for not more than 1 minute. It is then immediately withdrawn with a pair of chopsticks, dipped into one of the dipping sauces provided and eaten. These dipping sauces give flavour and character to the dish.

SAUCE 5
3 tablespoons sesame paste (or peanut butter)
2 tablespoons light soya sauce

3.2-3.5 L (13-14 cups) chicken stock
1 kg (2¼ lb) leg of lamb, cut into very thin slices 5 x 4 cm (2 x 1½ in)
500 g (1 lb) Chinese (celery) cabbage, cut into 5 cm (2 in) lengths

5-6 portions, for a family gathering or group of friends

Along with the dipping sauces, there should be several other prepared dishes for the diners to choose from.

This is a very warming experience on a winter's evening and you don't even have to venture as far as Mongolia or Beijing!

Method: To prepare the dipping sauces, mix the ingredients together for each sauce until well blended.

In a big, deep cooking pot, bring 2 L (8 cups) of stock to a rolling boil. As the stock is used up quite rapidly, at least another 1.2 L (5 cups) of stock should be kept in reserve for immediate replenishment as soon as the liquid in the cooking pot begins to run low. Add enough slices of lamb for each diner and cook for 1 minute. Remove lamb from stock. The diners then dip the cooked lamb in one of the dipping sauces. Repeat until all the lamb is used. Twelve platefuls of sliced lamb will last for about 45 minutes of continuous cooking by the diners.

When all the meat has been cooked, the stock in the pot will be rich and savoury. Add cabbage to broth in the pot. Cover, bring to a gentle boil, and lower the heat to simmer. Simmer for 8-10 minutes. The cover can then be removed and the soup ladled out into the individual bowls of the diners and drunk as a hot, refreshing broth!

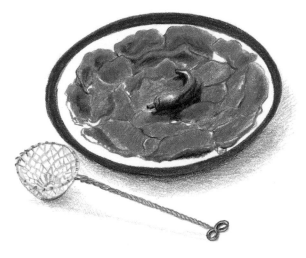

SLICED LAMB WITH LEEKS AND GARLIC

Dai Suan Yang Rou Pian

1 kg (2¼ lb) leg of lamb
Salt to taste
1 egg white, lightly beaten
2 tablespoons cornflour
  (cornstarch)
375 g (¾ lb) young leeks
4 tablespoons vegetable oil
4 slices root ginger, shredded
1 medium onion, thinly sliced
5 cloves garlic, crushed
3 tablespoons dark soya sauce
4 tablespoons chicken stock

5-6 portions

THE LAMB DISH I remember best from Beijing
(Peking) was the one I always encountered when
I entered the rickshaw-pullers' eating hut to obtain
a ride in the winters of the 1930s. As soon as I lifted
the heavily padded curtain to enter the hut, I was
greeted and nearly thrown back by the overpowering
smell of garlic. The dish which was being cooked was
Sliced Lamb with Leeks and Garlic.

Method: Cut lamb with a sharp knife into thin slices
5 x 4 cm (2 x 1½ in) in size. Sprinkle with salt, dip
in egg white and dust with cornflour. Clean leeks
thoroughly and cut diagonally into 5 cm (2 in)
sections.
  Heat the oil in a wok or a large frying pan.
When hot, add the ginger and onion, and stir-fry
over high heat for 1 minute. Add the garlic and lamb.
Continue to stir the contents over high heat for
2 minutes. Push away from the centre of the pan.
Add the leeks and stir-fry them for 1 minute over
medium heat. Pour the soya sauce and stock over
them. Stir the vegetables in the bubbling sauce for
45 seconds. Now stir in the lamb mixture and stir-fry
with the leeks over high heat for 2 minutes.

Serving: Serve on a well-heated serving plate for the
diners to help themselves.

INDEX

Aubergine *see* Eggplant

Basic beef broth, 22
Basic fried rice, 33
Basic red-cooked pork, 125
Basic steamed eggs, 80
Beancurd
    Beef broth and spinach soup, 24
    Cold-tossed, with pickles and dried prawns, 66
    Deep-fried, with bacon, mushrooms and eggs, 71
    With mushrooms and spring onions, stir-fried, 67
    Red-cooked, from the family kitchen, 70
    With sesame paste, 68
    Sichuan ma po, 69
    Stir-fried, with seafood, 72
Beef
    In black bean sauce with capsicums, 138
    Broth, basic, 22
    Broth and spinach soup with beancurd, 24
    With Cantonese rice noodles in black bean sauce, 45
    Cold-tossed, in mustard sauce with fresh coriander, 135
    Hot and sour soup, 19
    In oyster sauce with snow peas, 137
    Peppered, with onion, 139
    Red-cooked five spice, with turnips, 132
    And seafood with double-crisp noodles, 49
    Sichuan shredded, with carrots and celery, 136
    Sliced, in soft scrambled eggs, 134
Boiled rice, 32
Braised birthday noodles with red-cooked pork, 42
Broth *see* Soup
Buddhists' delight, 62–63

Cantonese barbecued pork, 131
Cantonese rice noodles with beef in black bean sauce, 45
Cantonese onion and ginger lobster, 97
Cantonese roast duck, 119
Chicken
    Drunken, 108
    Lemon, 110
    And mushroom soup, 21
    Paper-wrapped, 109
    Peking, in yellow bean sauce, 111
    Red-cooked, 113
    Rice, Hainan, 37
    Salt-buried crispy, 115
    Shanghai soya-and-ginger-glazed, 114
    Shangtung hand-shredded, 107
    Soup of three deliciousness, 26
    Soup with Chinese cabbage, 25
    Soup with noodles, 20
    In vinegar sauce, 111
    White-cut, 106
Chilli prawns, 93
Cold-tossed beef in mustard sauce with fresh coriander, 135
Cold-tossed beancurd with pickles and dried prawns, 66
Congee, 35
Crab in hot black bean sauce, 96
Crispy and aromatic duck, 118

Deep-fried beancurd with bacon, mushrooms and eggs, 71
Double-crisp noodles with beef and seafood, 49
Drunken chicken, 108
Duck
    Cantonese roast, 119
    Crispy and aromatic, 118
    Peking, 116–117

Egg-flower soup, 18
Eggplant, red-coooked, 57
Eggs
    Basic steamed, 80
    100-year-old, 78
    Salt, 78
    Soft scrambled, with sliced beef, 134
    Soya, 78
    Steamed, four varieties, 81
    Stir-fried omelette with tomatoes, 74
    Stirred, 73
    Tea, 78
    Wang Pu multi-layered omelette, 75
    With peppered prawns, stir-fried, 76
    With scallops, stir-fried, 95
Fish
    Peking sliced, in wine sauce, 98
    Red-cooked steaks, 88
    Sichuan bean paste, 90
    Squirrel, 99
    Steamed whole, 89
    Sweet and sour, 100
Four varieties of steamed eggs, 81
Fu Rong cauliflower, 82
Fu Rong Chinese cabbage, 83

Hainan chicken and rice, 37
Hot and sour soup, 19
Hot-tossed noodles with asparagus, 47

Lamb
    And leek Manchurian braised noodles, 43
    Mongolian hot pot, 140–141
    Red-cooked, with carrots and dried tangerine peel, 133
    Sliced, with leeks and garlic, 142
Lemon chicken, 110
Lion's head meatballs, 127

Mixed spring vegetable stew with bean thread noodles, 60
Mongolian hot pot, 140–141

Noodles
    Basic shredded pork chao mian, 41
    Braised birthday, with red-cooked pork, 42
    Cantonese Rce, with beef in black bean sauce, 45
    And chicken soup, 20
    Double-crisp, with beef and seafood, 49
    Hot-tossed, with asparagus, 47
    Manchurian braised, with lamb and leek, 43
    With mixed spring vegetable stew, 60

Peking ja jiang, 39
Shanghai cold-tossed, 40
Singapore rice-stick, 46
Ten treasure braised bean thread, 44
Three-mushroom, 48
Tossed in sesame paste, 38

100-year-old eggs, 78

Painted soup, 23
Paper-wrapped chicken, 109
Peking chicken in yellow bean sauce, 111
Peking duck, 116-117
Peking ja jiang noodles, 39
Peking sliced fish in wine sauce, 98
Peppered beef with onion, 139
Pork
　　see also Shredded pork
　　Basic red-cooked, 125
　　Cantonese barbecued, 131
　　Lion's head meatballs, 127
　　Red-cooked, with braised birthday noodles, 42
　　Red-cooked, with spinach, 126
　　Spare ribs, 129
　　Sweet and sour, 130
　　Twice-cooked, 128
　　White-cut garlic, 124
　　Yellow flower, 77
Prawns
　　Chilli, 93
　　Dried, with cold-tossed beancurd and pickles, 66
　　Dried and fresh, with green peas, stir-fried, 65
　　Peppered, with stir-fried eggs, 76
　　Stir-fried, king, 92
Pumpkin stew with tomatoes, peas and potatoes, 59

Red-cooked beancurd from the family kitchen, 70
Red-cooked chicken, 113
Red-cooked Chinese cabbage, 56
Red-cooked eggplant, 57
Red-cooked fish steaks, 88
Red-cooked five spice beef with turnips, 132
Red-cooked pork with spinach, 126
Red-cooked lamb with carrots and dried tangerine peel, 133
Red-cooked pork, basic, 125
Rice
　　Basic fried, 33
　　Boiled, 32
　　Congee, 35
　　Hainan chicken, 37
　　Savoury soft, 36
　　Yangzhou fried, 34

Salt-buried crispy chicken, 115
Salt eggs, 78
Savoury soft rice, 36
Seafood
　　And beef with double-crisp noodles, 49
　　And beancurd, stir-fried, 72
Shanghai cold-tossed noodles, 40
Shanghai soya-and-ginger-glazed chicken, 114
Shangtung hand-shredded chicken, 107

Shredded pork
　　Basic chao mian, 41
　　And Sichuan pickle soup with bean thread noodles, 27
　　With stir-fried bean sprouts and Sichuan pickles, 61
Shrimps *see* Prawns
Sichuan bean paste fish, 90
Sichuan chilli squid, 94
Sichuan ma po beancurd, 69
Sichuan shredded beef with carrots and celery, 136
Singapore rice-stick noodles, 46
Sliced beef in soft scrambled eggs, 134
Sliced lamb with leeks and garlic, 142
Soup
　　Basic beef broth, 22
　　Beef broth and spinach, with beancurd, 24
　　Chicken, with noodles, 20
　　Chicken and mushroom, 21
　　Egg-flower, 18
　　Hot and sour, 19
　　Lamb and leek Manchurian braised noodles, 43
　　Painted, 23
　　Shredded pork and Sichuan pickle soup with bean thread noodles, 27
　　Of three deliciousness, 26
　　Whole chicken, with Chinese cabbage, 25
Soya eggs, 78
Squirrel fish, 99
Steamed whole fish, 89
Stir-fried asparagus with garlic, 58
Stir-fried bean sprouts with Sichuan pickles and shredded pork, 61
Stir-fried beancurd with mushrooms and spring onions, 67
Stir-fried beancurd with seafood, 72
Stir-fried Chinese cabbage, 54
Stir-fried eggs with peppered prawns, 76
Stir-fried eggs with scallops, 95
Stir-fried green peas with dried and fresh prawns, 65
Stir-fried king prawns, 92
Stir-fried omelette with tomatoes, 74
Stir-fried spinach, 55
Stir-fry of dried and fresh mushrooms, 64
Stirred eggs, 73
Sweet and sour fish, 100
Sweet and sour pork, 130

Tea eggs, 78
Ten treasure braised bean thread noodles, 44
Three-mushroom noodles, 48
Tofu *see* Beancurd
Triple fry of three deliciousness with black beans, 91
Twice-cooked pork, 128

Wang Pu multi-layered omelette, 75
White-cut chicken, 106
White-cut garlic pork, 124
Whole chicken soup with Chinese cabbage, 25

Yangzhou fried rice, 34
Yellow flower pork, 77